UFOs
OVER POLAND

THE LAND OF HIGH STRANGENESS

Piotr Cielebiaś

UFOs OVER POLAND
The Land Of High Strangeness

By Piotr Cielebiaś

Edited by Philip Mantle

First edition published in 2015 by FLYING DISK PRESS

FLYING DISK PRESS
4 St Michaels Avenue
Pontefract
West Yorkshire
England
WF8 4QX

Published by
FLYING DISK PRESS

Designed and typeset by: Bob Tibbitts (iSET)
Cover artwork by Sebastian "Yoszko" Woszczyk

ISBN 978-0-9934928-0-8

Copyright © 2015 Piotr Cielebiaś. All rights reserved.
Without limiting the rights under copyright reserved above, no part of this publication
may be reproduced, stored in or introduced into a retrieval system, or transmitted
in any form by any means (electronic, mechanical, photocopying, recording or otherwise),
without the prior written permission of both the copyright owners
and the publishers of this book.

CONTENTS

PREFACE 1
EARLY SIGHTINGS.. 3
WARTIME UFO REPORTS 11
POSTWAR SIGHTNGS AND THE UFOLOGICAL MOVEMENT 17
UFO CRASH IN GDYNIA 25
FORGOTTEN YEARS.. 29
JAN WOLSKI'S CLOSE ENCOUNTER 35
HUMANOIDS IN PEOPLE'S POLAND..................................... 43
UFO ENCOUNTERS IN THE LATE PRP 53
PILOTS' ENCOUNTERS 61
MASS SIGHTINGS & GREAT FLYBYS 71
THE BĘDZIENICA-NOCKOWA INCIDENT 77
DECADE OF CONTROVERSIES – CASES FROM THE 1990's 81
EXOTIC BOOMERANGS AND FLYING TRIANGLES 91
FLYING SAUCER INCIDENTS OF 2010 103
POLICE OFFICERS GO ON RECORD..................................... 109
FORGOTTEN CRASHES AND THE JERZMANOWICE EVENT 115
USOs & UFOs OVER BALTIC SEA 121
UFO ABDUCTIONS IN POLAND... 127
THE GLINIK ANOMALOUS ZONE 137
THE CZĘSTOCHOWA UFO ZONE... 143

THE RZESZÓW UFO ZONE 151
FLYING HUMANOIDS... 159
CONSCIOUSNESS-RELATED CASES 165
SOME FINAL WORDS 173

ACKNOWLEDGEMENTS

I'D like to express my gratitude to a group of researchers without whom this book would not have been possible:

To Arek Miazga and Michał Kuśnierz – for sharing their UFO knowledge and collected UFO data. To Damian Trela, Arek Kocik, Grzegorz Tarczyński – for their work in collecting a huge amount of UFO data. I would also like to thank Marek Rymuszko, Wojtek Chudziński and "Nieznany Świat" – for their endless pursuit of information on UFOs and other fringe topics. To all those who are no longer active in the field of UFO research and to whom we owe so much.

I would especially like to mention Bronisław Rzepecki and Krzyztof Piechota, the late Zbigniew Blania-Bolnar and Kazimierz Bzowski – for their work in the creation of the Polish UFO movement and the collection of many UFO reports in the most "active" years.

A special thanks to Sebastian "Yoszko" Woszczyk – for his wonderful UFO artwork and cover design. We must not forget all the witnesses who have shared their experiences with me or my colleagues. And last but not least for Philip Mantle for his editorial work and patience.

PREFACE

THIS book is not about lights in the sky. It is about the land of high-strangeness.

It is also free from unnecessary deliberations and comprises mostly of facts and eyewitness accounts concerning things too weird to be mentioned in the mainstream media.

This book came into being as a reaction to the many predictable publications of contemporary UFO books and TV documents which contain mostly the same old cases, names and hypotheses. That tendency prompted many to assume that the best part of ufological history in Poland filled with spectacular and mysterious cases only happened in the 1970's and 1980's and that nothing new had happened since then.

In recent years only few UFO cases went public on international an level (as O'Hare saucer and the Stephenville lights in the USA) but on the other side *YouTube* and other websites are teeming with videos and reports, mostly anonymous and partially fake. The huge basin of knowledge called the Internet is slowly turning into source of useless or disordered information and disinformation and is not an accurate too to use for UFO research although it can be helpful at times.

Some skeptics and media outlets even preach that ufology is dead but here in this book we will show that this is simply not true. It simply needs money, new cases and dedicated researchers. In every country mysterious things still happen and deepen the UFO mystery. In Europe, Americas and Asia there are still active research groups doing excellent job but their results would be never known in the international UFO community if they were published in languages other than English. Due to the same mechanism you've probably never heard of 95% of cases contained in this book.

To sum up, we like syntheses but don't like to write entrances to syntheses. So in the preface we cannot give you a summary of the whole UFO enigma.

Regardless of this, decades of research have shown that the UFO enigma is an extremely complex issue that needs multidisciplinary studies. The UFO community is on the wrong track when trying to transfer their mindsets to intelligence(s) steering the UFO phenomenon. We like Jacques Vallée's word *metalogic* for characterisation of the *mentality* standing behind UFO activity and agree with his conclusion that the many forms that the UFO phenomenon takes may be equally important as beliefs and ideas it produces.

As we said, most of close encounters and other perplexing cases revealing the complicated nature of UFO phenomenon contained in this book have been never known in the West. Polish people also form part of the Western World although we prefer to be in the middle with the Eastern Europeans. Many things we will mention here may sound exotic for some readers. One of the things that may shock you is that the modern Polish era of close encounters with *flying discs* started in 1922. The book is a kind of historical essay on Polish UFO sightings compiled from ufological literature and my own work and research. It may be even called a kind of unstructured lexicon containing the most reliable, famous and bizarre Polish close encounters cases since the ancient Slavonic times to 2014.

As a historian and culture expert by education, I have tried to contain here as many eyewitnesses reports as it was possible and mixed them with other valuable (and digestible) information about Poland, its inhabitants, history and mentality. So let's start our trip to weirdest mysteries of that country…

Chapter 1

EARLY SIGHTINGS

Fiery demons • Examples of living folklore • Polish King sees UFO
Suspected balloons • Warsaw close encounter in the 1920's
The Ujazd UFO landing

UFOs in Old Slavonic Lore

A POPULAR trend in ufology tries to draw parallels between mythology, folklore and contemporary UFO reports. Data compiled and analysed by Dr. Jacques Vallée shows that there exists intriguing similarities between beings and phenomena from old folklore tales and modern accounts of close encounters. They are not restricted to visual similarities between *miraculous stars* or *gods' chariots* and *flying saucers* but also the aftereffects of encountering such phenomenon. There is a common thread in many tales and myths leaving those who were touched by *mysterious forces* (in the form of a dwarf, gnome, angel, god etc.) to never be the same again. They became mystified and confused by what they had encountered just the same as modern UFO experiencers (contactees/abductees and close encounter witnesses).

With an adequate dose of imagination one can also find ufological features in old Slavonic beliefs and religion.

Polish people are part of the Slavonic family including Russians, Czechs, Slovaks, Ukrainians, Belarusian, Serbs, Croats, Bosnians and other nations (who still can understand each others language to some extent). In the early Middle Ages our ancestors dispersed over Eastern and South-Eastern Europe laying the foundation for first states. Poland – state of Polanie tribe – appeared in the 10th century but the current historical theses assume that an earlier state of the Wiślanie tribe had existed in southern part of today's country (where Krakow is located) already in the 8th century.

All Slavonic tribes shared similar beliefs and in the well known scholar Andrzej Szyjewski's opinion, each group honored their own gods while there were also some universal deities for all. One of them was a four-faced Światowit (literally *one who see the world*) and Weles or Wołos – chthonic deity who was probably depicted as a Wildman (his name is connected with word meaning *hair*). Unfortunately, that's all we know about these Polish tribes' religion. After the conversion to Christianity in 966, Roman Catholic priests destroyed all relics and banned traditions devoted to the old Gods. They were so eager in their work that almost no archeological relics of ancient Slavonic places of worship survived. The Catholic Church is therefore responsible for a cultural and historical holocaust of Polish identity that even in today's modern era they refuse to admit to.

Part of pagan traditions and beliefs fortunately survived amongst the common people and there is the room where one can localise some veiled references to UFOs. Although we think that any intense search for parallels between traditional beliefs and ufology would lead to misinterpretations, there is one thing in old Polish folklore that bore a direct resemblance to term *unidentified flying object*. It is known under different names all over the country. The most common are *Ognik* (literally *flame*) or *Świetlik* (lit. *firefly*).

Researchers have met people of older generations who have witnessed unidentified flying objects and tended to describe them just as *Ogniks*. For example, after the second word war (WW2) an adult woman from the Częstochowa area described an evening close encounter with a huge luminous sphere emitting '*crackling*' sounds. She took it for one of those fiery objects she had heard of, interpreting her encounter from a folkloristic perspective. Therefore there is an open possibility that some reports of Ogniks might stem from incidents that can be compared with modern UFO encounters. The rest without doubt were the so called '*ghost lights*' – the Polish version of *will-of-the-wisp*.

Another noteworthy folklorist theme refers to Płanetnicy – *the sky people* who come with the wind and occasionally fall to Earth: "They are usually described as male beings of old age dressed in linen cloth. Other descriptions characterise them in a different way as small, sexless monsters or beings with body of a child and the head of an old man". Details of this can be located in the work of Adam and Barbara Podgórscy – authors of an excellent lexicon of Polish folk demonology.

For people skilled in ufology-folklore comparisons to the above-mentioned paragraph needs no comment.

Bogdan Baranowski (1915-93) – another well known folklorist stated that memories relating to old demonology sadly started to fade away after WW2 when new a socialist government, fighting with illiteracy and backwardness of people in the Polish countryside, initiated a program of cultural and social modernisation. Folk tales and spooky stories eventually landed on the scrap heap and those who believed in them were deemed to be *behind the times*.

However I have come across many reports suggesting that some tales of '*ghost lights*' and mysterious beings may stem from real encounters. People who shared them were living proof to Vallée's hypothesis concerning the link of old lore with modern UFO reports.

Some time back I spoke with people living in the vicinity of Sokole Góry Preserve near Czestochowa who in the 1980's had observed a number of unexplained lights *dancing* over fields in a most unusual manner. The sighting couldn't be explained in conventional a way so they assumed that it was the *Świetlik* that according to legends used to haunt that area. In 2004 in the same localisation a rectangular, bright UFO was seen in daytime. Perhaps there is a link between the two sightings?

In 1969, between Pieńsk and Lasów a group of young people returning from the cinema met with a weird glowing being that appeared under an oak tree. It is described as having a featureless gray head, light-blue torso (dress?) and hovered just over the ground. The group rushed toward the entity and gave chase. If the encounter had taken place some decades earlier, it would be surely interpreted as an apparition on angelic intervention the main witness, Marian B., reported. (His full report is contained in the chapter on flying humanoids.)

The *Dziennik Zachodni* (*Western Daily*) published an

An artist's interpretation of the famous flying humanoid encounter in Lasów in 1969. A group of witnesses met a strange luminous entity on the roadside and gave chase. The sighting would perhaps have been classified as a religious apparition if it had happened some decades earlier due to the being's 'angelic' appearance. (Credit: Sebastian "Yoszko" Woszczyk")

account of a man from Southern Poland who in his boyhood (probably in the 1950s) met with exotic *devil-like beings*. When his parents went to work in the fields he stayed home to guard the property. At some point he turned the radio on and heard *weird 'cracking' sound*. When he realised the same noise was coming from outside, he looked out of the window and saw a pair of strange, skinny beings with gray skin and huge eyes. Not surprisingly he then apparently passed out. He was completely shocked by what he had observed and the encounter stayed with him for the rest of his life. He assumed that the beings he saw must be *devils of some kind* (very popular in Polish folk tales) since he didn't know anything about UFOs at that time in his life.

Similar reports show that some people can still asses their ufological experiences from a religious or folkloric perspective. But it may be very hard to determine to which extent UFOs provoked the birth of original beliefs and myths (either Slavonic or other). It is a wholly speculative matter although there are some thought provoking stories preserved in ancient traditions and publications. But there are modern examples too. Such a confusion of UFO sightings as religious apparitions in fact occurred in 1984 when a man from Lisiec Mały near Konin saw a spherical UFO with a vertical dash inside in the vicinity of a local shrine to the Virgin Mary. He took it for a celestial sign (a kind of "divine eye") and builds a UFO memorial next to the religious figure.

Let us complete these deliberations with old Polish saying that *every fairy tale contains a grain of truth*.

Historical UFOs

The earliest Polish historical records featuring *anomalous aerial phenomena* can be traced to the medieval period. Those reports are deeply set in the cultural and mental context of that era. They are mostly scant chroniclers' tracks describing miraculous events in the form of *eerie comets, stars* or *signs* seen in the skies. It is worth mentioning that Polish people of successive eras were literally obsessed with astronomy and other occult arts so they were skilled in examining the skies very carefully awaiting celestial omens with the *tailed star* as being the most disturbing one of them all.

Many complex descriptions appeared in the 17th century – a period of great upheaval for Poland then called Rzeczpospolita (Polish for Latin *res publica – public domain* or *republic*). After unification with the Great Duchy of Lithuania it became one of the strongest European countries but simultaneously engaged in almost permanent conflicts with Sweden, Russia, Cossacks, Turkey and Crimea Khanate that left it depopulated, economically devastated and politically factious. In

1618 in the Szczecin area (northwestern tip of today's Poland, then under German domination) a young goat herder of German descent, Klaus Neuman, experienced a bizarre encounter with a small man who appeared out of a *'flying light'*:

> "He observed a weird light in the sky and then something resembling a dove came down and transformed itself into a four year old boy dressed in a white shirt who talked with the witness. After a while the boy disappeared and the herder saw above him something resembling an ascending star although the skies were entirely covered with clouds". This account was published by Jerzy Podralski in his article on Polish historical UFO reports in Głos Szczeciński (1979). This same author also found records of another incident from 1637:

> "At about 3 a.m. a brightly illuminated white spot was seen over Szczecin. Then a fiery object appeared in the middle of it. It was red at the bottom and white at the top. This object was ejecting huge beams of fire and red strings all around it. It moved erratically and at one point it descended over a mill and then a guard house prompting the soldiers therein to run outside."

A letter of the last great Polish king, Jan III Sobieski (1629-96) from 1683 provides what would seem like a very reliable account on unidentified flying object. The monarch who was engaged in a great battle with the Turks, who had started to besiege Vienna, wrote to his wife:

> "We saw in the skies about 7am in the morning, in pristine and very bright weather, something resembling a small rainbow formed into shape that was similar to the moon seen several days after the new moon phase. The thing was extraordinary. We were heading west while it appeared behind us, then turned east, at left from the sun. Then something like x or u began emerging from that quasi-moon. It all lasted for about half an hour."

The first modern reports on unidentified aerial phenomena come from the 19th century from Szczebrzeszyn and Pisz where meteorologist noticed *rings and fiery pillars pulsating with light*. A very interesting report from the end of the 19th century was discovered by Arek Miazga, a UFO researcher from the Rzeszów area. In the *Czas* newspaper from April 20th 1892 a reporter wrote a note about strange (and purely ufological) sighting that took place Przemyśl in south-eastern tip of Poland, then a part of Austro-Hungary.

> "In the last Saturday there was observed in Przemyśl a bright point that appeared over Jarosław, in the north-eastern direction. That object was spherical in shape and threw out of itself, both upwards and downwards, shafts of lights of electrical radiance and conical form. With binoculars it became clear that it was neither planet nor star since it was hovering in the air

about 0.4 miles over the surface and became circling area of about 2.5-3 miles in radius. So it may be assumed that was a balloon which the crew tried to do some reconnaissance with electrical lamp."

The journalist's effort to explain this anomaly with the *balloon lamp theory* makes him the precursor of modern UFO skepticism. But what is interesting, the same hypothesis accompanied another reports from Rzeszów where early in 1913 a strange object had been observed twice. As *Głos Rzeszowski* reported, the one seen in July was casting *beams of light down* on the buildings below and quickly disappeared into distance.

Such reports were the building blocks for the modern UFO era. However in Poland the UFO era had not begun after the Second World War but much earlier, just after regaining its independence in 1918…

Modern pre-war reports

The first modern Polish report on strange flying object, in my opinion, symbolically starting the country's modern UFO era, comes from the Warsaw district of Targówek and details a close range sighting of a saucer-shaped craft that took place in June or July 1922.

"I was strolling in Targówek with my brother-in-law and auntie when we saw something descending from the sky accompanied by a whistling noise" – the witness stated. *"We were sure that it would crash down but in some way that thing managed to stop in the air, 6.5 or 10 ft above the ground. It was enormous, a slightly flattened ball-shape, looking like two plates connected together by their upper rims. It looked as if made of aluminum, kind of silvery but also somewhat gray metal. I was observing the mysterious construction from 330-500 ft distance. Trying to catch a glimpse, I noticed that both parts of that saucer were separated by a kind of rotating ring. Other parts of the craft remained motionless. Soon the moving circle also stopped and I saw something resembling a frame – probably a part of the crafts windows. I got the impression that the objects crew was observing the onlookers. Then I was sure that the craft is going to touch down and we would enter inside but after a while it shot up at an angle of around 45 degrees. A loud blast followed. The above mentioned event was witnessed by hundreds of people."*

The Targówek case was described in Bronisław Rzepecki's and Krzysztof Piechota's book *UFO over Poland* (1996). Both authors (unfortunately already inactive in the field) started their research work in 1970's when there still existed generations remembering WW1 and the rebirth of an independent Poland. Previously the country was divided into three by Russia, Prussia and Austria who occupied Polish provinces for more than 120 years. The biggest part (with Warsaw) was annexed by the Russian Empire that then spanned from Polish Kalisz and Częstochowa in the west to Alaska in the east.

But let us return to the point. Rzepecki and Piechota obtained some other reports on classic UFO sightings that took place before 1947. One of the most unusual involved a possible landing with occupants seen outside the craft in 1926 or 1927.

> *"On August 23rd 1989 I met with Zofia L. and interviewed her about the incident"* – Rzepecki wrote in his book Close Encounters with UFOs in Poland (1995). *The incident took place in the meadows between Brzezie and Ujazd near Zabierzów (Kraków area). The witness was at that time fourteen years of age. On that day, at about 3 pm., she went outside to tend the cows belonging to her family. Suddenly the animals stopped and pulled on their chains forcing her to turn back. She looked toward Ujazd and saw some 650 feet away, three spherical objects standing on the ground or hovering just above it and in front of each stood a small being. The objects according to her were of the same color as cement. On each vertical lines were visible, interpreted by the witness as opened parts of the objects. The occupants were in her opinion smaller than her and dressed in greenish uniforms."*

Of the early Polish UFO reports I have chosen the ones that seem to be consistent with modern day accounts. The true scale of the phenomenon from the latter part of 19th century to end of 1930s is impossible to evaluate since we are lacking adequate reference points. Due to lack of public discourse on similar phenomena, witnesses avoided sending their accounts to press. Only decades after, when the UFO phenomenon obtained a degree of media coverage, did they contact ufologists saying: *We saw something like this too.*

Regardless of the true nature of UFO phenomenon – whether it is more paranormal as John Keel says or purely extraterrestrial as Stanton Friedman would argue – it seems that there are enough cases to officially push the border of the modern UFO era back before 1947. This step is not just symbolic and but also has serious implications for the understanding of the UFO phenomenon. There are those who try to explain it with the simplest of means state that *flying saucers* are just a cultural product of the Cold War and the Space Race. But cases as those presented above prove that the phenomenon existed long before the present hypotheses on it ever appeared and no matter what UFOs may be they were around long before the Cold War for certain.

Quotation sources

Szyjewski A., *Religia Słowian*, Kraków 2003.

Podgórscy B. and A., *Mitologia Śląska*, Katowice 2011.

Piechota K., Rzepecki B., *UFO nad Polską*, Białystok 1996.

Rzepecki K., *Bliskie spotkania z UFO w Polsce*, Tarnów 1995.

Miazga A., *UFO nad Podkarpaciem*, Ropczyce 2013 (ebook).

Podralski J., *UFO w Średniowieczu, Głos Szczeciński, July 09th 1979.*

Czas, issue of April 20th 1892.

Chapter 2

WARTIME UFO REPORTS

How 22% of Poles disappeared • UFO Landing in Nowiny
Spherical wonder over burning Ghetto • Rotating shield on the battlefield
Foo-Fighter seen from ground level

POLISH history is in fact one perpetual war tale but any other conflict was not as devastating and cruel as WW2. It is without a doubt the most traumatic period in Polish history. Attacked by German forces on September 1st 1939, the country was soon left out in the cold by its western allies and an inept government fled to Romania while the war campaign was still proceeding.

German troops had no mercy for civilians from the very outset of hostilities. With murder and robbery they tried to destroy the entire nation. Mass extermination of Polish Jews, mass executions, forced evictions, extermination of hundreds of thousands of Polish intellectuals and academics, cultural genocide, systematic robbing of museums and the destruction of King's Castle in Warsaw, forced labour camps and civilian massacres – all of this and much more took place during 5 years of occupation that took life of 22% of the Polish population. It is always good to remember such madness especially while sat in front of the TV watching another National Geographic documentary on the amazing Third Reich and its mysterious *Führer*...

But there is of course room for UFOs even in the chain of great calamities such as the German invasion of Poland which began WW2. Most UFO enthusiasts would link wartime UFO reports with the famous 'foo-fighters' – the alleged predecessors of flying saucers in form of ghostly lights playing cat and mice with airmen of both Allies and Axis powers. However in the annals of Polish ufology there exist some extraordinary (and unknown abroad) reports on UFOs from the period of 1939-45, with some sightings recorded during combat.

The Nowiny landing (1943/44)

This peculiar incident comes from archives of UFO researchers Piechota and Rzepecki. In 1987 they met the sole living witness of that event (from 5 original participants) who was 16 at time of the encounter. It took place in 1943 or 1944 in the small village of Nowiny in Chełm area (eastern Poland). The researchers were unable to set out the exact beginning of the incident although it probably started when a strange object touched down 110 yards away from witnesses' hut. Two people decided to approach mushroom-shaped UFO, finally being able to get very close and met its strange passengers.

"The object resembled a hat set on a wide bollard, i.e. it was a semi-circular cabin attached to a cylinder below. The hemisphere possessed a row of windows while the hole in the cylinder had a sliding door and a small ladder. The objects height was about 11 ft, while the cylinder was 3 ft high and about 13 ft wide" – wrote the authors.

The witness remembered that there were 8 or 9 beings near the object. Their appearance and behavior was very typical for post-war accounts. The Nowiny humanoids were about 4.5 ft tall and generally resembled humans. Their skin was of a pinkish hue but when they smiled the corners of their mouths formed an eerie half-moon shape. They wore headgear strapped below their chins as well as two-pieced outfits.

"Their language sounded like Japanese – was shrill and incomprehensible. With gestures the beings tried to force the people to enter their craft but the two witnesses refused (also with gestures). Finally one of the humanoids waved his hand causing the both men to tumble to the floor. Just after that occupants get onboard the craft it hissed, vibrated and then – accompanied by loud buzz – ascended vertically and departed at an angle into the sky."

Kazimierz Bzowski's sighting (1943)

Kazimierz Bzowski (1925-2005) was a prominent though controversial ufologist and publicist from Warsaw. At some stage in his career he realised that unexplained objects cannot be fully understood within the realms of conventional science and so he decided to examine certain UFO hot-spots with the controversial use of dowsing, in Poland termed as radiesthesia. With the help of engineer Miłosław Wilk, he formulated a theory trying to connect unidentified objects' activity with changes in subtle Earth energies. It was nearly as complicated as relativity theory so only a few people properly understood the concept. It postulated in brief, that the planet is surrounded with an energetic web dotted with holes (so called *stitches*) that allow anomalous objects to manifest.

Bzowski fought in the Warsaw Uprising during WW2 (1944) but a year before, while observing German activities as a scout of the u*nderground movement* during the Nazi pacification of the Ghetto in Warsaw, 18-year-old *Kazik* saw something that changed his life and probably inspired his ufological work which he undertook many years later.

It was April 9th 1943, just more than a week before an eruption of the Jewish uprising against the Nazis. Bzowski along with his companions tried to reconnoiter the whereabouts of German forces, watching a sector of the Ghetto consumed by flames. At about 5 pm they unexpectedly noticed an *airborne* object approaching the area and decided to examine it closer with binoculars.

"It was a sphere with sharply marked edges inside of which there were merging and entangled strips of two colors visible: raspberry-like and dark green-bluish. The object moved erratically through the air and it repeatedly was ascending and then descending. As experienced scouts they determined that it was moving with speed of German Fieseler Stoch airplane, i.e. up to 60 miles per hour."

Bzowski, who described his encounter in *UFO over Us* (2002), estimated that the object was passing about 200 ft in the air and was more than 25 ft in diameter but the most interesting part of their sighting was yet to unfold.

"Germans and Lithuanian gunmen who shot at people appearing in windows of the burning houses (not rebels but those who tried to escape fire) almost simultaneously stopped when the sphere emerged out of the smoke and closed their positions on Bonifraterska Street – a sector well visible to Bzowski and the onlookers from the German forces. All the soldiers fired at this sphere and the shooting went on for several minutes. Bzowski reported seeing bullets apparently passing right through the sphere without causing it any damage at all. The sphere was still floating above them and then it altered its course and headed towards the Old Town. Before long it stopped dead in the sky, shot off at a tremendous speed and disappeared from view."

Red UFO during the battle of Wielopole

The sighting of a *fiery shield* took place in the summer 1944 in Czudec (podkarpackie) and was witnessed by K. Marcus who described it in a letter to *Nieznany Świat* magazine. On that day along with his brother and father who was a veteran of WW1, they rushed to observe the on-going battle for Wielopole Skrzyńskie located on a hill approximately 9.3 miles away.

Marcus remembered the sight of fiery streaks of bullets although on that occasion the battle was rather quiet. Realising that there was not a lot to watch at the time the boys and their father decided to return home but then something very unusual appeared in the air.

> "It was getting late when from behind the southern hills a brick-red shield appeared. Having a diameter of half of the full moon, it was flying from south to north, flying at the level of the hilltops (650-820 ft) with a constant speed and horizontal flight. But it was rotating on its way and that gave me impression that it was 'rolling'. A full turn or roll of the object lasted about 2 seconds. The shield was of very intense color but was dull (i.e. not bright or radiating). The valley where I still live is about 4.9 miles wide and it took 15-20 seconds for the object to pass over it. When we asked father – an experienced bombardier from WW1 and gunner from Polish-Bolshevik War, he seemed perplexed. He said that it might be an artillery flare but it was impossible such a thing could be in horizontal flight."

Foo-Fighter seen from ground level

The elusive so-called foo-fighters – mysterious spheres of light that haunted WW2 airmen in the final years of the conflict were not the only elements of war-lore. Reports varied but in December 1944 Allied Headquarters in Paris issued a statement that those sightings might indicate that the German Luftwaffe was testing some new kinds of aerial weaponry. Their fears were fortunately unjustified and there were no reports of hostile behavior from these phantom lights. But on the other hand, it seemed obvious that some seemed to be intelligently controlled.

The Polish contribution to the foo-fighter legend is quite extensive. The first historical sighting of a greenish ball engaged in strange maneuvers over the Indian Ocean was reported in September 1941 by the crew of a Polish transport vessel the S.S. Pulaski shipping British soldiers. Also Michael Bentine (1922-96) – British comedian and actor who for some time served in the RAF Royal Air Force), mentioned interviewing airmen from Polish squadrons who saw those strange objects during a mission over the German testing ground at Pennemunde.

Polish ufologists have gathered some additional accounts on foo-fighters. The most interesting case came from the archive of Andrzej Trepka and was reported by Mr. Zenon Sergisz who made a daytime UFO sighting during the Warsaw Uprising in mid-August 1944. At about 11 am, during an interval in combat operations, he was admiring the clear and sunny weather. Suddenly his attention was drawn by a huge German bomber and three small points in the sky reflecting the Suns rays. When the aircraft departed, Sergisz had the impression that those objects began to descend. In seconds they lowered their altitude to such extent that they disappeared behind some nearby buildings but soon began rising up at an angle and vanished once again.

"Completely puzzled by these observations it was clearly the weirdest squadron that Zenon Sergisz had ever seen. The bomber was about 1600 ft above the city and just below it (maybe dozens of feet above the ground) those strange objects were making their way in a reversed flight unit. They looked like flattened spheres, smaller than the airplane and resembling something between a lens and a coin" – the witness reported.

Whatever they were, those objects seemed to mimic the foo-fighters strategy of toying with the aircraft without attacking them. Other wartime Polish UFO encounters involved sightings in Warsaw (1942), Częstochowa (1944) and Ostrzeszów (1945) but they were less complex or known from *second-hand* accounts. The abovementioned reports with multiple witnesses involved phenomena that without doubt can be classified as UFOs or even *flying discs* (as in Marcus' or Sergisz's accounts).

In his book *Operation Trojan Horse* John Keel wrote that the modern saucer era was directly preceded by a wave of *ghost rockets* over Scandinavia. But reports from Polish ufological archives coming from non-anonymous, reliable people who met with unknown aerial anomalies of other-than-natural origin, undoubtedly cast some new light on the UFO mystery as a whole.

The whole UFO affair, in its currently accepted form, had of course begun much earlier. 1947 was only the start of the official response to it with the sighting by Kenneth Arnold in the USA hitting the headlines and seeing the birth of the term "flying saucer".

QUOTATION SOURCES

Piechota K., Rzepecki B., *UFO nad Polską*, Białystok 1996.

Rzepecki K., *Bliskie spotkania z UFO w Polsce*, Tarnów 1995.

Miazga A., *UFO nad Podkarpaciem*, Ropczyce 2013 (ebook).

Trepka A., *Latające spodki nad Polską, „Wieczór wybrzeża"*, January-February 1979 (series of articles).

Bzowski K., *UFO nad Nami*, Warszawa 2002 (ebook).

Chapter 3

POSTWAR SIGHTINGS AND THE UFOLOGICAL MOVEMENT

Shy episode of UFO madness • Flying discs of the postwar era • Girl who touched a UFO • Abduction in the woods • Dr. Kowalczewski's photo

ALTHOUGH the first modern sighting of a UFO in Poland took place in 1922, initial publications dealing with anomalous aerial phenomena of non-natural origin appeared in newspapers in the middle of the 1950s, in the period of cultural *Thaw* after Stalin's death. Author of those articles, Kazimierz Zalewski and the other researcher of those days Andrzej Trepka were real pioneers of ufology in Poland. The outburst of interest in UFOs occurred in the late 1950s when the press – although fully controlled by the state – began to regularly publish reports on the phenomenon. The UFO problem had been regarded by the conservative and materialism-oriented part of Polish society as kind of whim or extravaganza but soon eyewitnesses' letters flooding the editorial offices forced some to change their minds.

During the first decade after the war was a tough time in Poland. It involved a change of the political system to socialism and accession to the Eastern Block. Stalinism in Poland was a period of political struggle that many apposed. But the most serious problem was the country devastation and the need of reform in many different areas. Whatever was said in the West regarding Polish socialism, in fact it succeeded in rebuilding and modernising the country and society on a mass scale. From a backward agricultural country ruled by military coterie of the pre-war era, Poland entered into industrial and fully modern times of course at the cost of dependence from the Soviet Union. Nevertheless the People's Republic of Poland (PRP) was called *the merriest barrack in the socialistic camp*.

The atmosphere during the Stalinist era didn't allow for UFO research. This all changed after 1953 with the establishment of the Warsaw Treaty. In 1955 a closed door policy to any official response from the Polish government to the UFO problem was put in place. The Army and the Special Forces gathered and maybe even analysed some reports in respect of their significance to national security issues but all the results of any research and information were kept secret and shared only with comrades in Moscow.

That state of affairs survived up until 1989 when democratic reforms started but in fact the UFO subject still remains taboo for the Polish government even today. No Polish politician has ever commented publicly on unidentified objects but this will be clarified in later chapters of this book.

So Polish politicians remain silent on this subject but UFOs clearly do not adhere to any political stance. Unfortunately little is known of Polish sightings from directly from the post-war period. Most of the sighting reports remain in the archives of ufologists who are not so eager to share them with their colleagues. From the cases that we do know about we chose a few of the most interesting ones from the period 1946-1959. The second of these dates marks out a truly perplexing incident that gave birth to persistent legend of an alleged UFO crash in Gdynia port.

In 2011 the UFO researcher Arek Miazga from the Rzeszów area, interviewed Mrs. Zofia D. – woman in her 70-ties who claimed that just after the war she observed, along with group of other people, a golden disc emanating light that appeared over an orchard in Sanok (in south-eastern tip of Poland) in broad daylight. Despite of her age she still had very clear memories of the incident that involved an object describer as *"very different to the planes seen during the war"* – she said.

> *"It happened just after the war. I was then 10 or 12-year-old girl. It was in the Old Town where we lived. There was an orchard and on that day an elderly man – its owner, came there to pick some plums. Suddenly, he shouted at us: 'People, come and take a look!'*
>
> *There was a kind of craft there, quite low in the air, entirely red and it looked like the Sun although much more flattened. Many people saw it but it was so long ago... It was maneuvering around the sky, going up and down again and again"* – reported Zofia D. who didn't remember how and when the UFO departed.

On August 16th 1949, a young girl from Wola Drzewiecka (łód/kie) on her way home saw strange a dark-greenish object she compared to *"two bowls joined together at the outer rims"*, and it was around 5ft in diameter. Its surface was smooth and resembled cast metal (without seams, holes etc.). Being curious the girl approached the object and…

> "I stretched out my right arm and delicately touched the metallic surface of the object with my index finger. I could feel slight vibrations coming from the object. From today's perspective it reminds me of an electrical shock. Quickly pulling back my arm, I noticed that my fingertip was reddened as if it had been burnt. I looked at the object and heard a quiet, metallic sound. The object began to rotate and rose up. Then it disappeared at an altitude of about 50 ft. But before it was gone, in the distance I saw very big and bright sphere the size of the setting sun. The object I touched departed southward, in the direction of the road connecting Drzewce and Słupia, where that sphere hung in the sky. The encounter with the metallic object lasted about 3 minutes but the mentioned orb stayed in that place for several days (!). My father said that it was a balloon but I couldn't remember seeing it in motion. At dusk it seemed to be getting dimmer" – she wrote in 1982.

Is it possible for an unknown object to remain in one place for such a long time like this orb? Unfortunately nothing more is known about that Close Encounter case though the witness claimed that she had very sharp and clear memories of the incident. Another girl who in 1954 approached a long metallic object in the woods remembered only a part of her experience. She was found unconscious in a clearing remembering that she went aboard a cylindrical craft with strange crewmen. Only scant details are available unfortunately.

That early UFO abductions (predating Villas-Boas' and Hills' cases) took place in the summer of 1954 in Węgierska Górka (śląskie) – a village in the southern Poland highlands. UFO researcher Rzepecki wrote that he came across the incident in 1986. The witness, E.W., then 11 years of age, along with other children, decided to go mushroom picking. (It is a very popular pastime activity all over the country). She could remember that suddenly something ordered her mentally to separate from the group and rush to a nearby 330 ft wide clearing. Soon she found herself there and noticed a huge, metallic, tube-shaped object hovering just over the ground with an opening in the hull which she immediately walked towards with a kind of mechanical, involuntary gait. "Going toward the object, she saw a being standing motionless in the doorway. It was 5.5 ft in height and had white facial skin and eyes resembling those of humans. There was a tight-fitting outfit covering its entire body revealing only the face. It also appeared to have some kind of *lump* on its back. The inner part of the craft looked like *polished aluminum* and contained four *panels* attached to the walls with humanoids manipulating each one. These beings were smaller than the other one measuring about 5 ft tall and wore gray overalls. After about a minute she received a telepathic message ordering her to sit down 2 ft away from an ash-gray, dull, metallic pillar reaching from floor to ceiling of the room. That was the last thing she remembered."

Despite the detailed description and a fact that case from Węgierska Górka (lit. *Hungarian Knoll*) predates Villas-Boas and the Hills, it cannot be compared with them firstly because too much time had passed between the incident and registration process. In fact even the emergence of the story was a bit suspicious. Rzepecki wrote that he came across the case during an interview with E.W.'s husband who witnessed a UFO sighting. During this interview she said rather unexpectedly that she also saw something of this kind and even visited the craft. Rzepecki noted that the woman began talking about cosmic consciousness and other subjects which suggested she knew more about the subject than she admitted to. It is still an interesting account and one that should not be dismissed out of hand.

The newspaper *Echo Krakowa* reported that on November 4th 1957, at about 7:30 pm, many local residents observed a *disc* the size of one-third half moon (the moon being already visible in the sky). On the 10th of November people from Skaryszew (mazowieckie) – where the biggest horse market in Europe is held – noticed a huge cigar of radiant colors that slowly traveled west making the locals very excited – noted Jerzy Domański in his leaflet on flying saucers. Some weeks after that incident, a red moving light scared people in Bielsko-Biała (śląskie). As the witness, Elżbieta Kuśnierz said, its light was so intense that the snow in the area was illuminated with burgundy tint. It seemed that the Beskidy region, where also Bielsko-Biała is located, was experiencing an intensive UFO flap. Among other reports there is that of Mr. R.G.'s account who observed from the balcony of his house in Milówka three symmetrical spheres in January 1957.

From the same period comes a very interesting note by Julian Zieliński from the Rodaki village in region of Jura:

"*On the nights of 22nd and 23rd January 1957, between 10:05 pm and 1:25 am, a terrifying thing can be seen in the sky. Six fiery, horizontal pillars ran from west to east. Three of them returned on the second night. The phenomenon was witnessed by crowd of people.*" Along with Grzegorz Tarczyński, I located the only living witnesses to this incident, Mrs. Zofia Oruba and Mr. Julian's daughter but it was impossible to determine if the sighting was caused by rare atmospheric phenomenon or real anomalous event. Mrs. Oruba nevertheless remembered that the objects were in *apparent motion* and not stationary.

Among the pre-1959 reports there is also a special case that provided one of the first and equally the best photographic evidence that stimulated serious press debate on flying saucers.

Dr. Kowalczewski's photo

Dr. Stanisław Kowalczewski, MD, lived in Warsaw. During the Christmas break, on 22nd December 1959 he took a fascinating photo in Muszyna – a popular resort

The famous Dr. Kowalczewski's UFO photo snapped in Muszyna in December 1958. This luminous mass when first viewed was thought to be the Sun but the photographer soon realised otherwise. The witness (now deceased) sent the picture to a number of newspapers in Warsaw. The original photo unfortunately went missing. (Credit: Stanisław Kowalczewski).

near the border with present day Slovakia. After returning home, he sent a letter with his account of the strange experience to two Warsaw newspapers.

"I spent the Christmas of 1958 on a two-week vacation in Muszyna near Krynica. At first the weather was very poor – for three days in a row it was dark and rainy. On the 4th day, i.e. December 22nd, the sun appeared at last. At about 3 pm, while I was looking out of the window towards the Poprad Valley, I suddenly noticed a yellow-orange cloud directly opposite the window. I thought it's a unique chance to get a very good photo of the area I focused on the Poprad River and the mountain in the background. Unfortunately there was a pole in the way and it appears in the center of the photo. After a short while some kind of yellow-orange sun emerged from behind the clouds. Seeing it, I immediately photographed the scene but I was not that confident that I had captured this phenomenon on film. I doubted if the photo would turn out. I began observation of thus sun and it turned out that it was quickly moving toward a cloud located just across from it. The weird hue of the object also drew my attention. Usually the setting sun is redder and bigger. At some point my wife interrupted the observation saying: 'The sun has appeared. Let's go for a walk.' Noticing my lingering, she hurried me along. Seeing the strange sun setting behind a cloud, I finally turned back and left the room.

Anyway, I was very surprised with the sight of the real sun in the hotel yard. It was located to the right from the previous one and, moreover, it wasn't setting at all. So what was the phenomenon I had seen and photographed before? Unfortunately the orange cloud disappeared and only the real sun shone happily over the area. Walking down the lane along the railway I recalled that in the last issue of Dookoła świata magazine there was a mention of something like a flying saucer as well as interview with a village woman who allegedly observed a big ball. That thing I saw also reminded me of a ball but was slightly flattened. So was it a flying saucer? To check this I had to get this photo developed. I got it four days later and was surprised to see a strange flattened oval shadow over the horizon with some bulge in the upper part hovering directly in the place where the strange phenomenon was seen. I said to my wife on the way back from the photo-shop that the strange shadow was surely a flying saucer seen on that day but she remarked that it is just a stain. My opinion was different. I remember the situation very well but why did the dazzling object appear on the photo as a dark one? That riddle needed to be solved. I was too shocked by the phenomenon to keep silent. It provoked in me some kind of inner turmoil."

Stolica (The Capital City) magazine editors, after obtaining the photo, sent a request to a specialist. Soon Zalewski's opinion appeared in the magazine stating unequivocally:

> *"With 99 percent certainty, I can say that the photo depicts a flying saucer and it is very similar to photos of similar photos from abroad. It is clear that the object was emitting its own light otherwise it could not appear on the photo as a uniformly dark stain with rounded edges."*

Prior to that, *Życie Warszawy* (*Warsaw Life*) published Kowalczewski's report along with opinions of two photo experts who analysed the original film. They excluded fakery but were unable to explain why the object that seemed to be a luminous sphere appeared on the photo as a black saucer-like aerial vessel.

QUOTATIONS SOURCES

Piechota K., Rzepecki B., *UFO nad Polską*, Białystok 1996.

Rzepecki K., *Bliskie spotkania z UFO w Polsce*, Tarnów 1995.

Miazga A., *UFO nad Podkarpaciem*, Ropczyce 2013 (ebook).

Znicz L., *Goście z kosmosu. Nieznane obiekty latające*, v. 1, Gdańsk 1983.

Domański J., *Zagadka epoki*, Warszawa 1979.

Zieliński J., *Kronika gromady Rodaki,* manuscript.

Stolica, #7/1959.

Chapter 4

UFO CRASH IN GDYNIA

*Gdynia crash was a real event • Flaming barrel and other descriptions
Alleged UFO photo • Object retrieved • Non-human being on the beach
Critics • Strange declaration*

THE year 1959 is symbolic in Polish ufology marking out seemingly the most important incident of that era – the legendary UFO crash in Gdynia port. The truth behind this history is very complicated as in other alleged UFO crashes. In the very beginning we can say with a degree of certainty that something did indeed plunge into the frosty morning waters of the port basin but the rest is not so simple to appraise…

There are three main sources of information on the Gdynia crash. First and most important involves press reports and eyewitnesses' accounts – the only factual material in this case. The other group contains very dubious information from sources abroad, alleging that an alien being was found on the Baltic beach by marine guards. The third source is the contemporary folklore which gave birth to the legend of the *Polish Roswell* based on things heard or seen by *this* or *that*, him or her but always anonymous witness.

On January 21st 1959, at about six in the morning, dock workers in the Gdynia port heard a piercing metallic sound also described by Jan Roczyński and Tadeusz Mikusiński as a *clear rasp sound rather like the friction between two metal elements.* Jan Blok who worked onboard the Jarosław *Dąbrowski* ship noticed State Police searching for something that had allegedly fallen into the waters of the port basin. "The thing passed just over my head. It was big, sort of pinkish in color, with a broad but not too long, fiery tail. Before I stood back that *weird thing* disappeared into water" – he said. Jan Kuczyński, a lift operator, said the object was about 3ft long, semicircular and pink, then gradually reddening in color.

Other descriptions involve comparisons to a *cone* or even a *flaming barrel*. The object fell into the 4th basin of the Gdynia Port. Another lift operator, Stanisław Kołodziejski, stated that the object evidently disturbed the waters surface. There were many other people who saw the object in flight and their reports appeared in *Wieczór Wybrzeża* (*Coast Evening*) newspaper.

> *"Włodzimierz and Jadwiga Płonczkier from Gdynia at about 6:05 am saw in the north-western portion of the sky a flying saucer of circular shape. It was an orange color with pinkish borders. After a while it disappeared behind local buildings".*

This was in a statement dated January 23rd. The dates of Płonczkier's sighting and other dockworkers' reports varied. It might be result of an editorial mistake but arguably there's a possibility of UFOs being observed over a longer period over Gdynia in 1959.

Persistent rumors and informational chaos gave birth to various unconfirmed stories. The most popular one is that an object that allegedly hovered over the port for several days after the crash was looking for a *lost companion*. Another rumor states that the exotic object was pulled out of the water and confiscated by the Polish military and later sent on to Moscow. When the era of Internet began, even some alleged photos of the incident emerged! Typing *Gdynia UFO* in to Google Images will reveal some black-white photos of a luminous body over an unidentified structure that may resemble the port in question. The photo in fact comes from Bzowski's archive and depicts an alleged UFO not over Gdynia but over Warsaw instead.

A meteorite impact was the top-rated conventional explanation for the mysterious crash report. Andrzej S. Pilski, MA – a specialist in space rocks wrote in 1999 that the Gdynia event was caused by an *iron meteorite* that embedded itself in to the muddy bottom of the basin and would be never located. However it turned out that there is a port employee who knows all the mysteries of the Gdynian UFO. Engineer Alojzy Data reported:

> *"It was a cylindrical container made as if of glass film, filled with a ginger substance heavier than water. Our laboratory staff was afraid of checking it. You know, after WW2 the seabed was littered with all kinds of filth such as phosgene or mustard gas. But the problem solved itself: a man from the Security Service appeared and simply took it away."*

The legend of an alleged alien survivor found on a Baltic Beach was born a long way from Gdynia. Its roots can be traced to Arthur Shuttlewood's book *The Flying Saucerers* (1978) that derived the story's source from a certain Antoni Szachnowski – an alleged Polish ufologist from London who in turn heard about it from a doctor examining the alien in Poland who then emigrated to UK (in fact no one heard about him Poland at all). The story says in short that a pair of coastguards encountered a strangely acting male figure who talked to them in an inconceivable language. Hospital examination showed that the stranger was probably non-human. It was determined that he had displaced internal organs and *additional fingers*. The being was in critical a condition so doctors needed to remove its ultra-durable metallic coverall. When they took off a kind of bracelet, the humanoid died.

This fantastic story gained a great deal of popularity and now it is an integral part of the Gdynia legend but Polish researchers are not so excited by its extraterrestrial interpretation. Although no one is questioning reports of Kołodziejski or Kuczyński, most researchers agree that it was probably a purely conventional object – probably a part of early satellite. As an example, writer and ufologist, Robert Leśniakiewicz, suggested that the alleged UFO was in fact a part of American SCORE suggesting that the legend on humanoid being was invented by Special Forces to satirise the incident.

This is not interpretation that I personally agree with. For me it was a natural-born legend and a cover-up wasn't necessary since the Gdynia story had been neglected for a long time. It was Bronisław Rzepecki who decided to reexamine and revise it, proving that something indeed crashed into the ice-cold waters in January 1959. But in his book, Rzepecki made also a very strange and controversial statement. "In November 1989, during a chance talk with an Air Force officer about UFOs, I found out that he read some reports on the Gdynia incident. He wasn't interested in ufology so only briefly looked at them but remembered details concerning the different physiology of the being and information that it remained alive for some time after it was recovered. The report not mentioned anything about its transportation to the Soviet Union but it remains unknown to the author of the report. It was *Top Secret*. I was unable to reach it, although I know where it's located (or rather where it was in the mid 80s.). Reliability of that institution as well as my informant suggests that the document addressed real factual events.

Superficial examination of the details of those two tales suggest that it's rather hard to combine the factual scenario of a small object plunging into the water and revealing some red liquid with the spurious story of a humanoid with polidactylism (extra fingers) wandering about on the beach. Legends and wishful thinking obscured the facts… or maybe Leśniakiewicz was correct with his idea of some kind of state sponsored disinformation. Moreover, according to some, the

1959 crash was the second one in Gdynia and third in row that took place on Polish territories. Data on them come from foreign sources and include an alleged crash-landing in 1943, during the German occupation, when a French worker came across a silvery object partially embedded in the sand. More information about that and several other alleged UFO crashes in Poland you will find in Chapter 16.

QUOTATIONS SOURCES

Piechota K., Rzepecki B., *UFO nad Polską*, Białystok 1996.

Rzepecki K., *Bliskie spotkania z UFO w Polsce*, Tarnów 1995.

Rzepecki B., *Incydent Gdyński*, „Wizje Peryferyjne", #1/1997.

Fryckowski M., *Katastrofa UFO w Gdyni. Legenda z ubiegłego wieku*, infra.org.pl.

Chapter 5

FORGOTTEN YEARS

Mass sighting over Warsaw • Early cases of flying triangles • Lampshades escorting a Volkswagen • Ethnologist's tale of the 'Oz factor'

IN 1961 the first Polish book featuring the UFO problem appeared. It was *Latające talerze* (*Flying saucers*) of Janusz Thor, published in the years of intensive public interest in the UFO subject. In the opinion of some Polish researchers, the next two decades (up to incident in Emilcin in 1978) was a period of ufological drought in Poland. Rzepecki and Piechota directly stated that it was a boring era with no cases at all of any relevance or interest. Their evidence of UFO sightings lists only a dozen cases in the 1960s and then a slight rise in the number of reports in the 1970's, paving the way for a large flap of sightings from 1978-1982.

Is this true that the 1960's were devoid of any significant UFO sightings in Poland? Surely not? My research has uncovered numerous interesting reports that remain available in various publications while other witnesses did not share their accounts until the 21st century. One of the most interesting episodes of UFO activity over Poland took place on June 30th 1961 when a bright spherical object appeared over Warsaw staying in place for several hours. Probably it was the first of several press-covered reports on mass UFO sighting in the Polish People's Republic.

UFO hovering over Warsaw

The newspaper Express Wieczorny (*Evening Express*) reproduced a reporter's photo of strange light *blob* hovering over Warsaw with the following information:

"On Friday afternoon inhabitants of Warsaw were buzzing with a 3-hour long sensational event. At about 7 pm lots of them noticed a large and bright thing in the sky. The rumor spread and soon all looked skyward, asking: 'Is

this Sputnik, a flying saucer or maybe a space rocket segment?' Controversies intensified when an aircraft appeared in vicinity of the object."

Reporters mentioned that they immediately called the local observatory and Air Force Command. According to the first hypotheses, it was a failed meteorological balloon that was falling back to Earth. But the National Institute of Hydrology and Meteorology stated that it was rather an unlikely solution. Despite the press information that the sighting lasted 3 hours, according to Piechota, the object remained in the air for around 8 hours, finally disappearing at 10:20 pm.

The ufologist in his article written for a now defunct UFO magazine paid attention to some intriguing elements in the eyewitnesses' accounts. According to estimations, the UFO that hovered very high in the sky and remained clearly visible significantly surpassed in size of the aircraft that came into view during the sighting. The account of Mr. Stanisław Saliński from Warsaw suggested that the Army was much more confused by the incident than was officially acknowledged.

"On that bright, cloudless day I was on my way home and at about 2 pm I went by Bielański Forest unexpectedly coming across soldiers who were searching the area in the scrubland. One of them replied to my question when I queried what they were looking for: 'I have no idea. They ordered us to search for some downed object'. Then over the woods I saw, very high in the air, a weird spherical object, intensely shining with colorful lights – from white to blue and red. It seemed to hover and was constantly whirling around with numerous flashing lights of different colors. I went for my binoculars and to my great amazement I saw that the object was moving as if in slow motion almost as if pushed by slight breeze. At about 3:30 pm it

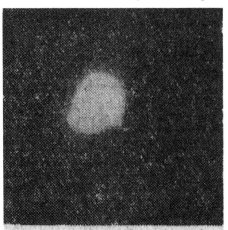

This is a press photograph of a huge UFO hovering over Warsaw in June 1961. The description below the photo describes the object as "a luminous balloon" although some witnesses said that it was too big and too structured for a balloon. Moreover, the object stayed over the city for approximately 8 hours. (Credit: "Express Wieczorny")

was passing directly over me. It disappeared at about 20:30 still emitting a strong light even after the sun had set. With binoculars I was able to discern that the object wasn't fully spherical. It was rather a polygon-shaped and not rotating at all, only the respective segments were changing colors constantly. The elements were also polygonal, somewhat like that of a soccer ball. To the west of me point there was the military airport of Bemowo. When the object began to be moving over that area, thee or four military aircraft took off and tried to intercept the object. The object was still hovering in the area at the time. . Moreover, when the aircraft were about nine-ten miles in the air, it could be estimated that the object was four or more times larger though it was probably about 18 miles above the ground" – the witness said.

In 2012 Arek Miazga received a letter of another witness who remembered this incident. As 10-year-old boy he observed a ball of bright color consisting of some rectangular elements that remained visible for quite some time. Then military MiG aircraft appeared in the area.

The Central press suggested that the object could also be a *Japanese communication balloon* that had escaped during technical work prior to the 1964 Olympic Games and then miraculously appeared thousands of miles west over the capital city of Poland.

Official explanations from meteorological and military experts were scant to say the least. Maybe they chose a wait-and-see policy before commenting, a tactic that may in fact have succeeded because the incident had quite literally been forgotten about. It is also hard to say what the soldiers were looking for in the Bielański Forest and whether it had any connection to the alleged separated part of the balloon with measuring instruments. Although close inspection of the object suggested that it was rather of anomalous origins, from some reasons the Air Force didn't decide to shoot it down possibly fearing that the debris (regardless of its origin) would crash into a populated area.

It must be said that some days after the sighting reports emerged stating that a local resident did indeed find a small balloons remains in his backyard. As in other controversial UFO cases, official explanations were not always properly adjusted to fit the facts of the incident in question leaving a great deal open to speculation.

Other interesting cases

Another two distinguishing cases from the forgotten years of Polish UFO history involve the first sightings of so-called 'flying triangles'. One comes from Dr. Vallée's book which claims that in 1959 in the Kołobrzeg area (Pomerania, on the Baltic Sea), Polish soldiers observed an object shaped like an isosceles triangle emerging from the water, rising up and making a lot of noise above the area before departing. Its length was estimated to be around 13 ft long. (The case is unknown in any Polish sources.)

The other story mentioned in Arek Miazga's book took place in the summer of 1968 in Rzeszów and was witnessed by three teenagers who noticed a triangular UFO flying over housing on Staszic Street. It was an *irregular triangle* emitting a soft buzzing noise and it flew slowly over the area heading in westerly direction. According to the witnesses account, it was barely visible due to its dark color though on the bottom part there were some bright colored '*bulges*'. Almost half a century later the same objects will be observed in Poland during a flap in 2013.

From 1966 to 1972 people residing in Dołhobrody (near Białystok) reported several sightings of a mushroom-shaped *light phenomenon* over the village, appearing both at night as in the daytime but unfortunately very little is known of these incidents. Another untypical case occurred in 1974 in Janowice and was witnessed by the family of Kazimierz Duda who rented a flat in a building of the village school. Duda said that on an autumn evening his attention was drawn to strange sounds that resembled static electricity. He went outside and saw a dark rectangular object standing behind the fence. On the surface of this very unusual object was a kind of '*dancing sparks*'. Fear in Mr. Kazimierz's mind was quickly replaced by a fierce curiosity. He decided to approach the object and even left his papers on the yard. But suddenly the *flying rectangle* started to ascend and stopped about 16ft above the ground, emanated very loud crack and intense sparks and then took off moving away at a curious angle.

In publication *Obecność UFO* (*UFO presence*) Zbigniew Blania-Bolnar about whom you will find out more in the next chapter, discussed a very intriguing close encounter that took place between Kargowa and Wolsztyn. On September 17th 1977 a honeymoon couple was on their way home from trip to Switzerland in their Volkswagen bus. Approaching Kargowa (around 2 am) they noticed two unusual lights but ignored them and continued to drive for another half a mile when something highly unusual took place.

> "An object in the form of two spheres approached us with enormous, indescribable speed and hovered over our car without disturbing the engine or any of the cars electrical systems. I stopped and tried to get a better look at the object. I can only compare it to two bright lampshades. One was slightly bigger than the other (measured less than a foot in diameter) and emitted a strong, white although not dazzling light. The other light was also intense but yellow-orange in color. Both the objects behaved as if they were bound together and stayed at a steady 6.5ft distance away from us. When I started the cars engine and drove away, both of the lampshades began pacing us parallel to the car."

The witness stated that he stopped the car to check the reaction of the UFOs that tracked them for about 6 miles in total, staying from 10 to 30 ft away from their car. The driver mentioned that he was nearly hypnotized by that encounter. In Wolsztyn, where the pair lived the *'lampshades'* rose up and departed at a very high speed.

There are yet still more examples of more classic encounters with flying saucers or *ogniks* as mentioned in the first chapter. Such an encounter occurred to Mr. Mieczysław Strzechowski – a well known Polish ethnologist who shared his story with me. In his very long account he detailed a close encounter with fiery ball that involved a short journey complete with an episode of 'missing time' and experience that has been termed the Oz factor by British ufologist Jenny Randles.

"It was in the first half of 1960's. I was a teenager, deemed in the local community as stable boy and a good student. On that day I was alone in our home. It was an old building so one needed to walk across all the building to put the lights on. While doing it I focused my attention on the window sill. It was always snow-white but then it began to get more and pinker. My curiosity changed to panic since that reminded me a series of fires. 'Fire!' – that was my first impression. Panicked I run out into the street. The street lanternes were turned off. I stopped and soon realised that it wasn't fire at all…

A sphere radiating with red light was slowly floating above me. Its surface wasn't smooth but seemed to be cut by some waving and maneuvering wrinkles. I saw its light reflecting off of ceramic parts of electrical poles that were nearby. I got an impression that it was alive! I watched it with my mind completely absorbed. I couldn't see nor hear anything. I was in some kind of stupor. I also couldn't the feel cold. The sphere slowly moved away and then began to gradually fade away" – Mr. Mieczysław said.

He added that looking at its surface he got impression that it was *"boiling like volcanic lava"*. But the most shocking aspect of that incident was the empty lifeless street that usually teemed with traffic. (It is this experience that Jenny Randles has termed the Oz factor).

"How could it be that only I witnessed this phenomenon? On the next day the city wasn't buzzing with rumors. In what sort of realm was I observing this sphere" – he asked.

Mr. Strzechowski's account was recorded in 2013 and it must be said that does not differentiate much from contemporary reports of this kind. It must also be noted that the atmosphere for public discussion on UFO experiences is still not very good in Poland. For some unknown reasons after Poland's accession to NATO in 1999,

UFOs became real taboo. It may be shocking for some, but it is more likely that you would encounter on the Polish TV news mentions of *miracles* resulting from prayers to a deceased Pope than reports on unidentified flying objects. Mainstream TV journalists who have become unbelievably stupid in recent years seek only the sensational news stories but for some unknown reason they refrain from covering credible UFO accounts. Witnesses who are brave enough to go public with their sightings in today's media in Poland risk a great deal of ridicule but myself and my colleagues will continue to support them in spite of this ridiculous attitude from the press and the public at large.

QUOTATIONS SOURCES

Piechota K., Rzepecki B., *UFO nad Polską*, Białystok 1996.

Piechota K., *Pierwsza po II Wojnie Światowej... fala UFO nad Polską*, "UFO", #3/1997.

Miazga A., *UFO nad Podkarpaciem*, Ropczyce 2013 (ebook).

Znicz L., *Goście z kosmosu. Nieznane obiekty latające*, v. 1, Gdańsk 1983.

Domański J., *Zagadka epoki*, Warszawa 1979.

Blana-Bolnar Z., *Obecność UFO*, Gdańsk 1983.

Chapter 6

JAN WOLSKI'S CLOSE ENCOUNTER

Life of Jan Wolski • Green-faced monsters and their original craft Examination • Popiołek's sighting • Was Blania-Bolnar a military agent? Controversies • Conclusions

THE nearly two decades-long period after the Gdynia crash was filled with many more spectacular UFO sightings. But none drew as much public attention as the Emilcin close encounter or as we prefer to call it, a *voluntary abduction* of 71-year-old farmer, Jan Wolski. It is hard to say whether or not his experience was part of large-scale flap of sightings or it was the trigger that encouraged people to become more open in sharing their UFO experiences.

From 1978 to the decline of the Polish People Republic in 1989, according to Piechota's and Rzepecki's estimates, there were more than 400 reported accounts of unidentified flying objects in Poland with 1979 as the *hottest year* (real number of sightings was probably much higher). They involved CE-2s, CE-3s and landings. Some of them were similar to Wolski's encounter while others were far more extraordinary although down the years many have sadly disappeared into obscurity. What is especially worth remembering is that Wolski was probably the first man in UFO abduction history who said *"Goodbye"* to non-human visitors.

That was a foggy day

The Emilcin incident is one of the few Polish UFO close encounters that has been published outside of Poland. The history of the complex investigation on this case is contained in three books by Zbigniew Blania-Bolnar (1948-2003) – its main researcher. It must be stressed that the Emilcin case caused much debate in the press and media that tended to have a negative effect regarding the witness' experience.

Jan Wolski and UFO craft from Emilcin – an artist's graphic reconstruction (from Zbigniew Blania-Bolnar Archives, contained in "UFO w Emilcinie")

However, right up until Wolski's death in 1991 no one was able to prove that he was hallucinating, lying or involved in some kind of hoax. Those who were in contact with him always described the elderly man in the same manner as honest, simple, reliable and straight talking.

On that memorable Wednesday, May 10th 1978, Wolski woke up early and went to visit one of the local farmers who possessed a stallion whose pedigree was deemed good enough to breed with Wolski's new horse. The morning weather was cold and soggy. Returning home, he decided to take a short cut along a road and pass through a forest lane. It was still early, the time being around 7.20 am. Driving his horse and cart (not a motor vehicle) through the woods he saw in the distance a number of silhouettes that he took at first to be scouts or hunters. But Wolski would describe the story in much greater detail.

> *"When they heard my horse and cart rumbling along the figures began to turn and look back towards me and when I got closer to them I saw their faces which appeared to green in color. I was surprised but I was continued to drive the cart. There is a small stream there, though at that time it was no more than a muddy pool. They tried to jump over the stream but one of them landed in it. Just after this they split apart and jumped on my cart as I was trying to pass*

by. They were not speaking to me but rather to each other and their language was very bizarre. I don't know how they could understand one another. When we talk, we do it slower but if we were to talk in that manner we would never be understood" – said Wolski, adding that the humanoids speech sounded like *t-t-t-t-t-t-t*.

Wolski was then a 71-year-old and had four sons some of whom were still living with him as they had yet to marry. He had graduated only three classes at elementary school but continued his education in a village school and also had some private home tutoring. His lifestyle was rather austere. In the period before the sighting he had neither radio nor TV set. His working days were filled with farm duties with an occasional holiday and a visit to the local church for leisure. Despite his lack of education and simple lifestyle Wolski was regarded as a very well-mannered man.

But let's return to his story.

"So I drove the cart to the bushes and as we passed them I noticed a 'bus' in the air! I was extremely surprised. I said to myself: 'What's going on!' It (the bus) was easily visible and was entirely white like a crystal. The road led me towards the craft so I tried to speed up trying to avoid it. At around 60 ft in front the craft one of the beings gestured me to stop. I wasn't afraid. I stopped the horse but it's an animal with such a character that it won't stop unless it wants to. So the being grasped the reins of the cart and helped me to stop it. Not surprisingly the horse then became a bit uneasy..."

Green men and their craft

Wolski wasn't afraid of the beings during the first encounter since they seemed delicate and were considerably small, about 4.5 ft in height. Although with their prominent cheek-bones and slanted eyes they resembled Asians seen by Wolski during the War. The skin of their faces and palms was of an oddly greenish-olive color. Their eyes were human-like, noses tiny and mouths in the form of a slit. The rest of their bodies was covered with tight-fitting dark outfits (resembling frog skin) connected with angular boots. They also had some lumps around the neck area.

The craft that hovered over the clearing looked like a big haversack – a cuboid with a convex roof and a kind of impeller on each side (resembling oblong drills). It was therefore *quite original* even by ufological standards. Wolski noticed that it generated some kind of a *'buzzing' sound* that made the horse feel very uneasy. In the hull of the craft there was an opening with something like *a swing* hanging below it. Soon Wolski discovered that this was an escalator – very stable despite its shaky appearance. Wolski stepped on to this escalator after being urged to do so by one of the beings. He was lifted up along with the alien to the craft that was now around 16 ft above them.

"Wolski stated that there were two identical beings inside the craft" – Blania-Bolnar wrote.

"One of them held in his hands an object resembling an icicle. Wolski was slightly pulled to the left by the being who had boarded the craft with him. He also observed a number of 'dark birds' (rooks in his opinion) lying on the floor that were still alive and moving but unable to stand up normally. With hand gestures the being who brought him onboard the craft gestured to Wolski to start to undress. He took off his coat, sweater and unbuttoned his shirt thinking that's enough but one being urged him to undress completely. Some of the beings then appeared in front of him with an item resembling two gray saucers that moved (joined or parted) emitting a 'clapping' sound."

Before Wolski had been submitted to any kind of examination he was offered a morsel of the mentioned *icicle* to eat but he politely refused. The green colored beings seemed to enjoy eating this icicle as he saw that they were chipping pieces from it and putting it into their mouths. In the meantime a fourth being entered the craft.

Mr. Wolski remembered that the interior of the UFO was very austere and cold. It was dark and devoid of any complicated equipment, *panels* or even lamps (the only source of light was the opening in the craft). The ceiling was just over Wolski's head. The only thing suggesting some king of technical operation involved one of the beings putting a *baton like device that was* topped with a ball into two holes in the wall (Wolski assumed that he was *regulating something*). There were also some simple benches set to into the walls. An acrid smell, hard to define, permeated the interior of the craft. Wolski said that to him it somewhat resembled the smell of sulfur.

"In the final part of the encounter he was ordered to put his clothes back on again in the form of yet more hand gestures and then with more gestures he was informed that he could now leave. Standing in the crafts door he turned around to look back, took off his cap and greeted the beings saying 'Goodbye!' (He said that would be bad manners not to bid them farewell)."

Apparently the four beings tried to mimic Wolski's movements and ended up with a grimace on their face according to the author Blania-Bolnar.

Blania-Bolnar arrives

The elevator took the farmer down to the ground and he left the clearing. Wolski was asked many times whether or not he was afraid during the encounter. He explained that he is a man of *cold blood* and an unbeliever in anything paranormal. The beings didn't seem hostile or aggressive but rather inquisitive instead. It has been suggested that Wolski himself was curious to see what was inside the craft. No matter how many times he was interviewed Wolski always told the same story and eventually he became tired of curiosity seekers and journalists who visited Emilcin.

Wolski returned home suffering a degree of mild shock that day on May 10th (at about 7:50 or 8:00am) Just a few minutes after the encounter he alerted his wife, Janina, his son Józef who with Boleslaw Miotła, their neighbor, ran to the nearby clearing sadly finding no craft but they did report seeing some unusual foot prints (on the grass, mud and in a molehill).

On May 25th Witold Wawrzonek a UFO enthusiast from Lublin, learned from his co-worker rumors relating to a *'frog-people's' landing* in the Opole Lubelskie area. Wawrzonek visited Emilcin, interviewed Wolski and then sent a letter to the national television and Zbigniew Blania-Bolnar – sociologist from Łódź and a ufologist who became the main researcher of the case. Zbigniew Blania-Bolnar published the results of his investigation in series of books with *Zdarzenie w Emilcinie* (*Emilcin encounter*) being the most detailed one. He dedicated it to Stanisław Lem – a world famous sci-fi writ and noted UFO skeptic.

Blania-Bolnar was assisted in his research by Dr. Ryszard Kietliński from the Łódź University Institute of Sociology along with psychiatrist Ryszard Krasilewicz and a team of doctors and biologists. They undertook tests to examine Wolski's memory and also his hearing abilities. The farmer was subjected to psychiatric and neurological testing, an IQ test, Thematic Apperception Test all of which failed to indicate that Wolski was either delusional or fantasy prone (full reports and opinions of researches Blania-Bolnar contained in his summary of Emilcin case). All of those involved in these tests suggested that Wolski had indeed experienced something of an *unidentified nature*.

It turned out that Wolski wasn't the only witness to this incident. At 8:00am in the morning on May 10th, Adam and Agnieszka Popiołek (respectively 6 and 4-year-old at the time) observed something extraordinary passing over their backyard. Their mother, Janina, while preparing them breakfast, heard a sound so weird and loud that she looked for the children to check if they were both okay. After a short while Adam appeared saying that he saw a *"strange plane similar to a bus"* with a *"green-faced pilot peering through a window"*.

According to researchers, Adam could not have invented this story based on rumors of Wolski's encounter (his sister was too small to be interviewed). Their reports, although different in form, in Blania-Bolnar's opinion described the same craft. Adam, for example, told insisted that *the soldier's* outfit was dark-grey and the *plane* had an object resembling a *plank* along its bottom part. Was it the elevator Wolski stepped on?

What about any other witnesses? Did others also hear strange *rumble sound as reported by* Janina Popiołek? It is possible that others either saw or heard the same but Blania-Bolnar was unable to find any other witnesses. Could it be that other witnesses were put off from coming forward by the ensuing press coverage? Even in Poland there is a stigma surrounding those who report such close encounter events.

Controversies

Though Wolski's account seemed sincere, some assumed that the village man was tricked in some way or had simply dreamt of the green men encounter and then took it be a real mysterious event. There were several scenarios proposed by the press. The first one involved a deliberate scouts' prank on the old farmer. The second being Wolski's incorrect interpretation and misidentification of a helicopter. The final scenario was that Wolski had vivid alcoholic hallucinations.

Blania-Bolnar made very strict observations of Wolski and also he conducted interviews with members of the local community who knew him. As a result he was convinced that Wolski would not misidentify a helicopter and he was not an alcoholic. It was also determined that on May 10th there were no helicopter flights in the area but the most importantly, Wolski was well acquainted with them. In the opinion of Blania-Bolnar, the number of details reported by the Emilcin witness indicated that he was a good observer and would not mistake a helicopter and crew in suits for that of non-human beings in a UFO.

> *"You should know that I came to the conclusion that I should have kept my mouth shut about it, but my neighbors spread the rumors that then went nation-wide..."* – remarked Wolski who was exhausted by constant interviews and media requests.

Other controversies relate to Blania-Bolnar himself who remains a mysterious, somewhat suspicious and rather unpopular person. Ufologists poured scorn on him claiming that he was arrogant and even called him an *agent* of the special services. His whereabouts and association with the State Police remains very unclear indeed but some researchers surely had their own personal reasons to try and defame Blania-Bolnar. His response to these unfounded accusations was sharp and abrupt even calling one researcher 'an ape'.

If the Emilcin encounter was indeed an extraterrestrial contact, Wolski with his polite manners and "*Goodbye*" made a very good impression!

Quotations sources

Blania-Bolnar Z., *Obecność UFO, v. 1.*, Gdańsk 1983.

Blania-Bolnar, *Zdarzenie w Emilcinie*, Łódź 1995.

Bzowski's group interview with Jan Wolski, TVP Archive.

Chapter 7

OTHER HUMANOID REPORTS IN POLAND

Echoes of Emilcin • Humanoid scares students in Przyrownica
Mushroom-picker encounter • Crooked astronauts in Człuchów
Humanoids from an endangered galaxy • The Czerniaków landing

A FLOOD of reports followed the Wolski case, many of which were yet more encounters with UFOs and their occupants. Three such reports echoed the Emilcin story and led to researchers discussing whether or not these reports had something in common or were connected in some way. There were two encounters that took place in Przyrownica (September 26-27th) and Golina (September 27th) in Central Poland. The first was in 1978 while the last one occurred in 1981 in the Hel Peninsula.

These first two encounters remain somewhat controversial and their credibility varies between different researchers. There were many other such cases reported although the information on the majority of them is somewhat scant. By far the most interesting and credible classic cases are the Człuchów (1979) and Czerniaków (1982) sightings. A considerable amount of high-strangeness reports and events involving flying humanoids has prompted me to describe them in separate chapters. But let us return to 1978 when Wolski's story became famous and was covered in the press and state-controlled media in the following months. Some (including Blania-Bolnar) expected that similar stories would emerge and be fabricated by people craving public attention during which he called 'the silly season'. But nothing like that occurred until late September when in the *Kurier Polski* (*Polish Courier*) a story emerged detailing a green-faced oddity seen by schoolchildren in Przyrownica.

Two encounters in one day

When Blania-Bolnar heard of this encounter he visited the children in question who had witnessed the encounter as well as their teachers. Sadly Blania-Bolnar had already made his mind up that the case was a fabrication even before he set off. In his opinion, children's story was inspired by a TV report on UFOs aired on Saturday, September 23rd.

"These children saw the green-men on the TV and then plotted this scenario" – Blania wrote, saying that the young witnesses had repeated some inaccurate information on the Emilcin beings features that he had deliberately published in his first report on Emilcin case as a trap for hoaxers (it was a small detail of the aliens' description concerning their outfits). If any alleged new witnesses duplicated them it would prove that they were either lying or confabulating by supporting this deliberately placed inaccurate information on the Emilcin case.

But when UFO researchers Rzepecki and Piechota visited the village in the Sieradz area (łódzkie), another different scenario of the encounter emerged. It turned out that the children's encounter was preceded by sightings of a red spherical UFO made on September 26th by Anastazja Bystra (retired teacher) and her daughter as well as Józef Pawlak, a local farmer. In his book *Bliskie spotkania z UFO w Polsce,* Rzepecki detailed the children's encounter that some found quite disturbing (some readers may find it similar to famous Ruwa UFO landing in 1994). He determined that at 8:00 am, on September 27th Katarzyna Kolińska was on her way to school from Magnusy when she unexpectedly noticed a bright outburst of light near Łysa Góra (lit. *Bald Mountain*), which lay close to where they lived.

School lessons started at 9am but the children that arrived earlier went to play in a small grove adjacent to the school. They returned to the classroom in great excitement, telling their teacher, Janina Chlebowska, that they had encountered a *strange man* in the woods. One of the boys had lost his shoe during the panic to escape. Before notifying the Militia, the teacher went with the apparently disturbed students to the location of encounter. One of the girls, Anna Jarocińska, decided to stay behind in school but soon, possibly afraid of being separated from the group, she followed them taking a wrong turn along way. Anna described an experience of an eye-to-eye encounter with a being whose face she described as a "featureless mask". This took place just approximately 160 yards from the school. Radek Wawrzyniak along with the Karolak brothers stated that they had seen the humanoid as they were in the front of the group. A 5.5ft tall humanoid with a green face and dark costume seemed to walking through the forest some 30 ft away from them. At one point it turned to face in their direction, probably in reaction to hearing their voices.

Rzepecki suggested that Blania-Bolnar for some unknown reasons decided to *discredit* the Przyrownica case declaring it as a fraud. None of the witnesses ever doubted their experience, even 11 years later when interviewed by Rzepecki, Piechota and their fellow researcher, Bogdan Grzywna they steadfastly stuck to their story. In their opinion there was no doubt that it was a real incident that went unnoticed by the press and was poorly researched at the time.

However on the same day, around 60 miles away from Przyrownica, Henryk Marciniak met similar humanoids during mushroom picking in Golina (wielkopolskie), at about 1pm. The incident turned out to be much more controversial though Blania-Bolnar who visited the witness deemed Marciniak's story authentic. This event first emerged in the local press that publicised the strange story of a 31-year-old driver.

The story went as so:

"I took my motorcycle and drove to pick some wild mushrooms in the forest. I parked my bike amongst the trees and searched the area. I decided to return home when I saw a 'shack'. At first I thought: 'When did they put that here?' It was standing on four supports and was around 110 yards away from me. Whoever had placed it in the forest went to great pains as the clearing was filled with tree stumps and the ground had also been ploughed. This type of operation would have required a crane and some form of transportation. But I hadn't seen anything. Realising this, I became slightly concerned" – Marciniak stated.

Curiosity getting the better of him he decided to examine the object. Suddenly its door opened and the witness saw two small individuals with *"unpleasant faces, resembling that of green frog"*. One of them gesticulated and Marciniak took it as a request to stop. In the meantime steps appeared from the object and the pair of humanoids descended.

"Now, when I'm thinking about it, I don't know whether I extend my arm automatically or due to fear. One of them approached, stopped just before me and looked into my eyes. He seemed hesitant but then made a step forward and extended his arm. The first one had empty hands but the other grasped something like a small camera. He first poked my motor bike seat with his finger and touched the brake while the other one was following him as if taking photos or something. Then the first being took my bag of mushrooms and looked at me. I pointed my finger first to the mushrooms and then to my mouth, trying to convey that it was something edible" – the witness said.

Marciniak then showed the curious aliens how to ride his bike but while doing this he heard strange buzzing sound coming from "the shack". It must have been some kind of alarm, because both beings went aboard immediately and started their vehicle. The shocked observer admired its ascent to treetop level and its quick departure which was preceded by a blast of steam from its hull.

According to his account the beings were only 4.5 ft tall, with greenish skin, protruding cheekbones and slanted eyes with dark-red pupils (The Emilcin humanoids were brown-eyed). Shaking hands with these beings (no matter how peculiar this may seem), the witness felt that their skin was cold and elastic. There were similarities with the case and that reported by Wolski. The apparatus they held in their hands looked like 'two plates' with a small box in front of it. Even the shape of the UFO was similar. Marciniak stated that the UFO was metallic, cuboid in shape, with a marked roof on one side and clear on the other.

Blania-Bolnar had no doubt that this story was authentic, but still very mysterious nonetheless. Marciniak claimed that just after the UFO departed he had a number of side effects. For the remainder of the day he felt very tired and lethargic. It must be pointed out that many years later Marciniak denied the story and didn't want any contact with anyone who was trying to research the incident. He simply wanted to be left alone. It remains a matter of debate of whether or not Marciniak made this later denial simply to be left alone which is not uncommon among UFO close encounter witnesses.

Welcome to Hel & the Czerniaków landing

Blania-Bolnar openly criticised UFO researcher Rzepecki in *Zdarzenie w Emilcinie* (1995) for exposing his peculiar methods of research. With two spectacular CE-3s within 5-6 hours of each other is still filled with many unanswered questions. But surely it is better for ufologists to ask searching questions rather than to simply accept things at face value. Questioning is a sign of thinking is it not?

Before a third was of sightings appeared after the Emilcin case we literally have a close encounter in Hel (the name of the village). An extremely intriguing event took place in the Człuchów (Pomorskie) area on August 10th 1979, at about 9 pm. On that day an anonymous woman was fishing in the bay of a local lake. While fishing the lady in question noticed someone was crossing the waters over a 100 ft from her. She at first took it be a poachers' boat but soon realised that it was soundless and moving far too quickly for a row boat. Slightly nervous, she shouted to her partner who was on the bank of the bay with his dogs. He too noticed the arrival of the strange boat and without thinking went to inspect it.

> "I took maybe a dozen steps towards the boat and was astonished to see two silhouetted figures some 60 ft away heading towards the road. My dogs must

A painting depicting the controversial Hel UFO encounter in 1981 made by the witness himself. (Credit: Ryszard K. / Kazimierz Bzowski's Archive)

have smelt something unusual and they rushed towards the figures. Those dogs were old and wise and one of them was a rather fierce beast. Unable to stop them, I watched both dogs approach the figures and then they retreated. I was surprised at this reaction from my dogs but nevertheless I knew that the nearby woods a relatively new addition to the area and I was afraid that strangers were going to trample on plants so I yelled: 'You can't go there, it is a prohibited area!' At the sound of my voice they turned and faced me" – the man reported.

But the following sight almost made the witness sick.

"The beings were about 5ft tall and dressed in something that resembled tight-fitting spacesuits. Both suits were dark and identical, not black but maybe dark-brown in color. I clearly saw the outline of both figures and the only visible features were some sort of visor at their eye level. This really puzzled me as the visors seemed to 'glitter'. But there were two other strange elements of the beings' appearance. First is that their upper arms were very close to their bodies while their forearms protruded sideways. Their waistline also seemed unnaturally broad. They also seemed to have no necks and had some sort of 'lumps' around the shoulder area" – the man said, adding that their legs seemed joined together, forcing the beings to walk like penguins.

It wasn't the end of the encounter though *crooked astronauts* disappeared from his sight. Just for a while the observer lost eye contact with them and soon they were gone! To his great amazement after the figures had been lost from view he saw a bluish-grey colored object in the shape of rectangle with rounded edges. Seeing it moving away he began to feel a little dizzy.

The witness of yet another event, Ryszard K, an artist from Warsaw, experienced a face-to-face encounter with more green colored humanoids. The beginning of this encounter was very similar to that of the Wolski encounter. A man on vacation was walking in the forest by the Baltic Sea. Up ahead of him on the path he observed a pair of jiggling boyish figures some 65 yards away. From this distance the figures appeared to be dressed in greenish colored uniforms, so he took them for boy scouts. Upon getting nearer they turned out instead to be men whose skin was colored green and had faces that reminded him of plastic masks.

The Hel Peninsula is the thin *appendage* on the northern tip of Poland and Hel city is a tiny spot on that appendage. *Hel is a hotspot* for tourists who flock there from all over the Poland, especially during the summer vacation. Ryszard K.'s encounter took place in the area of Chałupy – then a village (now district of Władysławowo city) that became famous because of local beach for naturists (nudists). The 38-year-old Ryszard K. said that on the day of his encounter he became bored with sitting around his camp and went for a walk with the aim of taking a few photographs (yes, he had a camera during the close encounter). He walked down the lane, overtaking some elderly tourists with a dog and then decided to take a photo of a dragonfly when he noticed the two beings for the first time. It seemed somewhat strange – he thought that they wore jackets despite the sweltering heat. For me here is the most interesting part of his detailed account that he shared with UFO researcher Bzowski:

"I walked several dozens yards and after a turn in the path I saw the two beings again. They had been straddling the footpath with slightly folded elbows looking like cowboys preparing to shoot. At that point I was only 12 yards from them. I became alternately hot and cold with amazement because suddenly I realised that they were not human beings. They were looking at me and vice versa, remaining motionless, like a couple of dolls, no more than 5 ft 5 inches tall, in dark green, tight-fitting outfits.

Their faces were an olive-greenish color, with big eyes with white parts looking the eyes of a human. But their mouths were just slits. They didn't seem hostile and kept calm so I decided to reach out and try to talk to them. I was just a few feet away from them when heard in my head sort of communication from them: "Don't speak, go ahead". At the same moment I noticed a strange, spindly craft in the forest behind them" – Ryszard K. explained.

He added that at some point the humanoids changed position without moving and he could feel stiffness on left side of his head. He was also able to watch the beings carefully, noticing dark 'boxes' on their waist belts and a yellow wrinkled strip on the abdominal part of their outfit. But in Ryszard K.'s account there were also some elements of the paranormal or of high-strangeness in nature.

"When I approached them for the first time, I saw some sort of mist covering their bodies from the top of their thighs to the middle of their torso. This mist seemed to emanate from the strange craft in the woods. As I went past them, I couldn't control my curiosity and turned back towards them. I saw them once again facing me. I also saw their craft but it seemed to be decreased by half in length!" – he added.

The observation of a UFO and its occupants turned out to be the least strange aspect of this close encounter. After a short while, and with his mind still trying to understand what had happened, he stopped walking and waited for the elderly couple he had seen earlier who surely must have caught him up by now.

"I saw the elderly couple approaching both of whom were immersed in conversation with each other. Their dog was sniffing around. I waited impatiently

for them to reach me but suddenly realised that the pair (and their dog) walked right through me literally as if I was a non-material being. I was paralysed with amazement and fear. 'Maybe I've just died' – I thought to myself but then I felt an agonising pain. I ran after them and caught them up. Grasping the old man's arm strongly I yelled: 'Haven't you seen me on the path, haven't you!' He tried to free himself from my grasp, poking a finger in the side of his forehead and murmuring something about 'nutcases'."

Bzowski tried to explain why the witness was not able to get a photo of the phenomenon. Ryszard K. explained that the mental transfer wasn't limited to just the one mentioned command. Some may take the following as a product of a fantasy-prone mind, but others may find the typical aftereffects of contact with a non-human intelligence. As he said, he entered some other state of consciousness and his attention was focused on the strange communication he had with the beings.

"I saw an extremely bright flaming star, spitting out flames like a giant stove. My mind interpreted this information showing that was a picture of a quasar in the home galaxy of the beings. Their home planet will be consumed by it within the next million years but they had already begun to search for new home for their civilisation. Earth and our Solar System are not an attractive location for them. But by accident they had left on our planet six members of their group. They asked me for help..." – Ryszard K. said, adding that after the encounter his point of view and area of interests changed considerably. Again this is not an uncommon after effect with those alleging a close encounter of this type.

The case might remain suspicious for some but Bzowski claimed that his group was able to identify the Chałupy UFO landing site which had seven impressions. It is alleged that the soil and plants in the impressions was compacted to such an extent that the soil felt as hard as rock in each impression. Bzowski described the case in the *Perspektywy* magazine and soon after publication two other witnesses came forward with accounts that might strengthen Ryszard K. story. One involved a *"strange, colorful cloud"* descending over the forest when the sighting occurred.

Some months after the incident, life in Poland was drastically altered by the introduction of martial law with an announcement in December 1981. The government of General Jaruzelski, trying to crush any political opposition and on the other side, to prevent Soviet intervention in Poland which might have resulted in real war, decided to imprison many of the Solidarność (Solidarity) political activists. There were also many restrictions for ordinary citizens involving a curfew, the sealing of borders, restricted access to some cities, mail censorship and so on. But no new laws or politics did not apparently apply to UFOs.

Somewhere in the now lost archive of Bzowski whose wife gave away after his death, there were many very interesting case files including the classic story of UFO landing in the Czerniaków district of Warsaw (famous for its folklore and music).

"It was a warm night from 29th to 30th of September (1982). However a radio weather forecast had predicted a frost so Mr. Władysław S. and his 12-year old son were forced to pick all the pears from the trees in their orchard located near Górka Czerniakowska (Czerniaków Hill) near Wolicka Street. They had been storing the fruit in a shack and their work dragged on to about 1:30 am – curfew time" – Bzowski wrote.

They lived in the local area so they decided make their home carefully as it was after curfew. Nearing the Social Insurance Institution building, they could smell smoke and being afraid of being caught outside after curfew the father and son hid in some nearby bushes. Soon they noticed something that caused them both to *"freeze"*.

"Less than 25 yards away, over a hollow part of the terrain, a strange object was hovering just about 3 ft from the ground. The object looked like a flattened loaf of bread some 20 ft in diameter. A faint orange glow was emanating from its underside causing the grass below to smolder.

There were two beings around the object. They seemed skinny and naked. One had its head lowered as if looking for something in the grass. The other projected a circle of light some 20cm in diameter which looked like an orange glow. The area was devoid of any sound at all. When the beings disappeared behind the object the two witnesses slowly began to withdraw."

Bzowski was able to establish that there was another witness – a militia officer who observed the UFO from a balcony.

Many other sightings occurred in the same era including those with *"missing time"* or alleged alien abductions. No one was able to answer what the humanoids were looking for or what was the real scale of the phenomenon. From today's perspective it is almost unbelievable to imagine that people would want to contact the news media saying they had witnessed something extraordinary and allow the publication of their name as well.

In the People's Republic Poland (PRP) era the press was strictly controlled by the government. Contacting it, UFO witnesses hoped to get some answers posed by their experiences. It is also noteworthy that journalists of that era were not as critical, skeptical and narrow minded as they are today.

QUOTATIONS SOURCES

Blania-Bolnar, *Zdarzenie w Emilcinie*, Łódź 1995.

Rzepecki K., *Bliskie spotkania z UFO w Polsce*, Tarnów 1995.

Piechota K., Rzepecki B., *UFO nad Polską*, Białystok 1996.

Turowski K., *Mieszkańcy kosmosu w Wielkopolsce*, Express Poznański, 06-08/10/1978.

Turowski K., *Kim była tajemnicza istota o zielonej twarzy?*, Kurier Polski, 03/10/1978.

Bzowski K., *UFO nad nami*, Warszawa 2002 (ebook).

Bzowski K., *Sieć Wilka*, Rybnik 2004.

Chapter 8

UFO ENCOUNTERS IN THE LATE PRP

Official opinions • Echoes of Fatima? • Wicie photos
Ambulance blocked by a UFO • Mother and child assaulted by flying saucer

IN the People's Republic of Poland UFOs were invading cities and towns, prompting the quick formalisation of UFO groups across the country. In five years after the Emilcin encounter, there appeared around thirteen new ufo research groups all over Poland, with Klub Kontaktów Kosmicznych (Club of Cosmic Contacts) led by the well known writer, Lucjan Znicz Sawicki (1923-2004) who for more than a decade published a newspaper column on UFOs and related phenomena. Every major city in the country got its own UFO group (some formal), conventions were held and publications abound. The PRP's government or People's Polish Army wasn't formally involved in any official research of the UFO phenomenon but as you will see in the next few chapters, some unofficial interest on an official level did exist.

Scientists decided to toe the official the line. An interesting effort was made by scientific writer and journalist, Bogdan Miś who in the late 1960's interviewed a group of Polish scientists concerning the subject of flying saucers. Eleven out of the eighteen of those interviewed assumed that the UFO enigma was a real phenomenon although of conventional origin. One anonymous responder stated that it was connected with some kind of extraterrestrial *intervention*. For most of society it was apparent that the UFO problem, whatever it was, must be the result of something the Soviet Union was doing. In fact, for a long time the most popular explanation for strange things seen in Polish skies was that they were witnesses advanced Soviet technology or even technology from other Western countries.

Unidentified Flying Objects had been encountered under many circumstances, sometimes untypical and amusing but often disturbing as well, posing a potential threat to the eyewitnesses in question. One of the most notable examples took place in 1979 when a circular object literally blocked the way of an ambulance with woman aboard who was about to give a birth.

Echoes of Fatima?

Much has been written about the legendary Miracle of the Sun witnessed in Fatima by a crowd of onlookers in October 1917. Prof. Joaquim Fernandes in his works collected many reports of reliable witnesses who described the object as a *rolling snowball* or *shield* clearly different than the real Sun. I am very interested in correlations between UFO encounters and Marian apparitions (visions of the Virgin Mary) which in my opinion deserve separate and meticulous study. But here is a curious fact. Although Poland is mostly catholic country and the Marian cult is widespread, there were very few mass apparition episodes in our history with probably Gietrzwałd (1877) as the sole example comparable to Fatima, Mediugorie and others. There are numerous reports about paranormal events bearing some resemblance to apparitions but not directly connected to those of the Virgin Mary.

Something that can be described as a secular equivalent of the Sun Miracle took (noted in many apparitions) took place in January 1979 in Słupsk (pomorskie) and was witnessed by Mr. Jerzy P. who forwarded me his long and detailed report in 2013, describing all aspects of his observation. It was undoubtedly a mass event and the witness heard reports of other sightings separate from this one.

On that frosty afternoon Mr. Jerzy – a designer in a shoe factory hastily left his studio and headed to the main factory building. Making his way across banks of snow, he looked up noticing that something was wrong with the Sun which was hanging in a completely cloudless and bright sky.

> *"It was (the Sun) suspiciously small and although its position was right (in the southern sector of the sky) it was also too high, as if in July. Then I realised that it was impossible for it to be in that place and it should have been more of a red colour and not so whitish. I took some steps in a south-westerly direction and could not believe my eyes. There was another sun"* – he reported.

Despite his inappropriate clothing, he decided to stay and diagnose which one was the real Sun. Soon a sequence of events happened that proved that it wasn't just a sundog (an astronomical phenomenon).

> *"They remained motionless for about a minute and then, at least, the suspicious Sun became increasingly greater in size. Then it overtook in size the real one that was on the left. It seemed huge. I started to think that it must be an object*

of some sort. Then it stopped to grow and slowly began to diminish. This whole episode lasted for around a minute or a little bit more. From my perspective it looked as if the object was moving away. When it was in the size of the rising planet Venus, there happened something that left me totally shocked. I understood that it could not be any physical object – a meteor, asteroid or some other celestial body lost in the Earth's atmosphere. Suddenly it made unbelievably dynamic, horizontal move to the right in some out-of-this-world manner, as if disobeying terrestrial laws of physics. It gained speed without ant apparent acceleration. It suggested to me that the object was in the control of some intelligence which possessed technologies capable of breaking the laws of physics."

Mr. Jerzy immediately reported the sighting to his co-workers but no one took it seriously. His encounter was one of many involving the same scenario that provoked so many questions about nature, measurements and the capability of these Unidentified Flying Objects. In 1957 a similar report from a highlander from Beskidy, during a UFO flap in the Żywiec area, saw something the he described as a "second, blood-red sun" that emanated light so strong to temporarily tinge the area with its color. It would seem that Mr. Jerzy's sighting was not unique after all.

Ambulance blocked by a UFO

What is known as the Tropy Sztumskie – Kalwa incident from September 5th 1979 was one of a few Polish UFO sightings that made an appearance in the international ufological press. It is also one of the few UFO encounters that posed a potential danger to the witnesses and also a case in which an object of unknown origin behaved as if it was actually trying to make contact. This incident included the sighting of a spherical object that blocked the path of an ambulance and led to a call for Police intervention. The UFO also seemed to have some sort of strange influence on the ambulance driver – Grzegorz Skoczyński. Other witnesses were paramedic Andrzej Olejnik (sitting on the passenger seat), Doctor Barbara Anaczkowska-Piazza and Elżbieta Pluta – the pregnant patient. The doctor was first to notice the object, then in form of red cloud, at about 3:30 am.

"It was something weird resembling a sunset. 'Tell me please what is that? It may be either the sun or the moon. But it can't be UFO' – I said to the driver. From the left side there was a red ball that then suddenly disappeared. I saw it again in the Tropy Sztumskie area. 'It was huge' – I remarked. It was an orange-red color, with sharp contours. I described it as a sphere but it could also have been a circle" – she said.

At about 3:45 they drove to the intersection at the Malbork-Dzieżgoń road and turned towards Kalwa. As the driver said, it remained clear as the object approached and was now running parallel with their vehicle. Skoczyński said that the UFO was maneuvering around all of the obstacles in its way and mimicked the ambulance's changes in speed. After a while it accelerated and overtook them, blocking their way. Shocked and confused Skoczyński stopped the ambulance just 165 yards away from UFO that was hovering a few yards over the road ahead. Then it dropped down to just a few feet above the ground.

> "We thought that this huge sphere was going to absorb the car. I shouted to the driver, urging him to turn the lights off because I thought that light is attracting the object. I noticed that it wasn't uniform in color. There were some lighter, yellowish patches on its surface. We all felt a little weird. Someone (maybe even me) remarked: 'It's UFO'. Then I told to patient: 'Try to not give a birth and stop looking at that!'"

Curiosity prevailed and Mrs. Pluta leaned over and sneaked a peak at the *thing*. Then she admitted that she could feel some kind of "radiation" coming from the object though she was undoubtedly the most concerned and excited of the entire group. The UFO glowed red but illuminated only a small patch of the asphalt below it with a white light. All the witnesses gave similar descriptions. Being wider than the road, it must have been more than twenty two feet in diameter. From this close up distance some previously unseen details were observed including two dark, horizontal bands on the objects surface (some five feet from the top and bottom of the sphere) and some kind of *lattice* covering, black in color. Skoczyński said they looked like "blood vessels on X-ray".

Although the sight was mesmerising, Mr. Anczkowska-Piazza didn't hesitate and ordered Skoczyński to turn back to the nearest railway crossing (just a few hundred yards away) which had two guards on duty who would also soon see that object. The final part of this encounter turned out to be equally astonishing. "At this point I turned radiotelephone on and called the operator, Teresa Cyran. There was no interference with the radio" – the doctor said. "She helped to inform the Militia that *this thing* was blocking our way. We asked them hurry up and get to our location. Skoczyński, the ambulance driver began to feel very odd. Perhaps it might have been caused by anxiety but I could not feel or see any symptoms to explain this. Then I returned my attention to the ambulance. The sphere was still balancing above the road for a further 10-15 minutes. Then it sharply turned aside. Continuing its maneuvers, the object had been gradually becoming less and less intense. It turned black in color very quickly. When we turned the lights of the ambulance back on, two-third of the sphere turned a deep red in color."

The whole sighting lasted about twenty minutes. After this period of time the witnesses described the UFO as becoming dimmer and according to Skoczyński, at some point it just took *off*. He turned off engine and went to inspect to see if the road ahead was passable. The UFO was now gone. He said that on the next day he searched the area for any potential traces but found nothing.

What would the Police officers have done if they had indeed arrived at the scene? Why did the Police decide not to react despite the potential danger to human life? And why did the object decide to block the f the ambulance. Was it a deliberate action or attempt of contact? We will never know the answers to these questions, of that I am certain.

Wicie mass sighting & photos

The Wicie incident provided one of the most interesting UFO photos from the era. It took place on September 3rd 1983 in the tourist resort in Wicie and involved the mass sighting of luminous object ejecting smaller ones. Photographs taken by Mr. Wiesław Machowski (then living in Zabrze) showing a hat-*like UFO* remains very popular but as I managed to establish in 2013, during contact with him, all previous reproductions in all publications were not accurate. Probably some editor rotated the Machowski photo to make the object look like a typical flying saucer. In fact, on the original photos, the UFO looks like a *hat standing on its brim*.

A luminous object over the Baltic Sea had been noticed for the first time by Machowski, his daughter and friend during fishing in a local coastal lake:

"On that day we had seen it three times. In the first instance it was in bright weather. I was fishing with a friend and suddenly, when I looked at the sea, I saw a beautiful orange sphere with another one below" – he said.

They had been keeping their eyes on the object from time to time for about thirty minutes. But when they returned to the boarding house, it appeared again but that time much closer to the coast. Excited, Machowski ran for his new Kiev camera and took three photos. It is quite possible that some of 150-200 guests that stayed there had a similar idea. Moreover, in the close vicinity there was another hotel.

"I remember that was the last day of good weather. All the guests admired the phenomenon while they were lying on their blankets sunbathing" – said Machowski who now lives in Stuttgart (Germany).

The full duration of the event was up to two hours! For all that time the same sequence had been repeating: the bigger light had been ejecting down a smaller one that was stopping at some height and returning to the *mothership*. Then the object disappeared for about twenty minutes but then returned being again much closer to the coast than before. After that it disappeared for good.

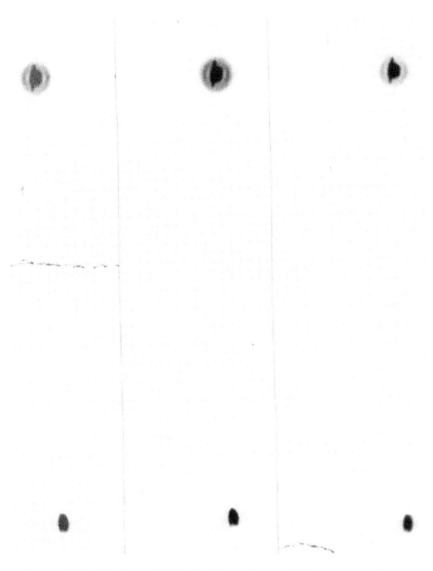

The set of Wicie UFO photos (1983) by Mr. Wiesław Machowski. This was a mass sighting of a hat-shaped luminous UFO that ejected a small spherical object. The UFO hovered at first over the Baltic Sea before moving off. On most reproductions, the UFO is wrongly depicted as a typical flying saucer. In fact, it looked instead like a hat standing on its brim. (Credit: Wiesław Machowski, photo published on infra.org.pl)

Mother and son assaulted by saucer

Arek Miazga researched a quite disturbing 1984 encounter of a mother and her child from the Podwisłocze district of Rzeszów. It occurred on a summer's day when Mr. Danuta (then aged 29) took his 2-year-old son to a local playground in the neighborhood next to a small grove. The sighting started unexpectedly when a *bright cupola* appeared in the background of the WSK motor factory. It was a metallic looking object that seemed to be getting closer and closer so the panicked woman picked up her child and ran to seek refuge. Standing behind a tree, she began to observer of very unusual spectacle.

"It was a big, round saucer with something akin to lamps around its perimeter, but lamps that did not emit any light. The object even brushed the tree top causing leafs to fall down. The noise from it became unbearable and it seemed that the object was going to crash to the ground. It had circled the area and began hovering in mid-air. It was just some 30-50 feet above the ground and its size was of a similar diameter. It was green-metallic in color. I was just terrified. I held my son in such a way to prevent him from seeing the thing. The lamps that I mentioned before were bulging. It was just matter of seconds. In short, it just came, circled the area and departed" – she said.

Arek interviewed the witness and persuaded her to reveal the story on a YouTube video. According to Mrs. Danuta, the cupola was about eight feet in height and had a slight *convexity to its* bottom part. What was interesting is that the UFO emitted a loud noise and also caused some damage to the tree tops. It changed its color from metallic to green. It has been speculated that this was some kind of camouflage.

Unfortunately, there were no other direct witnesses of the event as the area at the time was very sparsely populated. In the final part of sighting, the cupola headed toward nearby apartment houses and in matter of seconds, shot up and disappeared. Arek Miazga said that it was impossible for other people not to have seen the UFO but even Mrs. Danuta didn't share the details of her encounter until 2010 some twenty six years after it occurred.

Mrs. Danuta's story is just one example from a series of sightings in a city we call in *Polish UFO Pole.* Arek Miazga is doing an excellent job that resulted in his book *UFOs over Podkarpacie* (2013) of which the first volume is almost entirely devoted to incidents in Rzeszów and its region. It turned out that the majority of them are very similar one to another.

QUOTATIONS SOURCES

Piotr Cielebiaś and Michał Kuśnierz Archive / infra.org.pl

Arek Miazga Archive

Miazga A., UFO nad Podkarpaciem, Ropczyce 2013 (ebook).

Piechota K., Rzepecki B., *UFO nad Polską*, Białystok 1996.

Ryszkowski J., *Spotkanie z ognistą kulą*, *Panorama Północy*, #41/1979.

Chapter 9

PILOTS' ENCOUNTERS

UFO instructions for military pilots • What Col. Grundman (and father) know?
General Czernów sighting • Attempts to down UFOs
Sightings by groups of pilots • Airfield guard warned by UFO
Exciting encounter of Mr. Lubertowicz • Glider contra flying triangle

THE question of Poland's official reaction to the UFO problem cannot be discussed without cases of both military and civilian pilots who have encountered those objects. Polish ufological publications abound with similar reports that in the most remain unknown abroad and some originate from the PRP era. Below I present them in three separate sections on civilian and military pilots as well as military technical and other personnel sightings.

According to many military informants, The Polish Air Force of People's Polish Army issued a special protocol for potential UFO observers in uniform. Official *rules for those who work in flight control, command posts and air traffic as well as personnel actions in case of detection of unidentified flying objects*, obliged all military eyewitnesses to immediately report incidents to their superiors and to "follow strict safety rules during UFO tracking". It also advised them to keep their tongues under control.

Official *Polish government/military UFO files* remains a controversial topic. If these ever existed they were surely not related to any specific project on unidentified aerial phenomena. There is one man, col. Ryszard Grundman (1931-2015), who claims that he had been collecting such reports but purely on his own and that he was not part of any official UFO project. When he retired, his files contained several dozen cases from the PRP period all of which disappeared under mysterious circumstances.

"When I was the chief of Air Traffic Services of Air Force and Air Defense in the 1980's, I often received reports on objects demonstrating unexplained behavior. Up until my retirement in 1992, I collected as least several dozen reports. All of them landed in a special folder marked as unexplained cases. Along with Col. Jerzy Topolnicki who was then my direct Commander, I tried to examine and analyse them but it was hard to do anything with just a mere report from a pilot. But we did come to the conclusion that even if we do not understand this phenomenon, it may eventually turn out to be fully explainable in the future. I could not turn a blind eye on events that would be potentially dangerous to our flight security. It was my mission to keep them watching" – he said in an interview in 2009.

Polish military reports on UFOs are probably scattered around a variety of official archives. But the most important question is: *What was official military response to unidentified objects at a higher level?* It is possible that Air Forces of the Warsaw Treaty nations looked for decisions or suggestions from *The Big Brother's* command in Moscow. Soviet officials indeed run several projects devoted to UFOs, including one named *SETKA* (*Net*) but their results officially were the same as their American counterparts. This being that UFOs were of no interest and that all official UFO investigations had ceased.

Undoubtedly from a military standpoint the most important feature was the potential hostility of these objects and risks they could pose to national security. The reports and cases contained below show that the Air Force reacted to UFOs presence in the best possible way. However, the nature of that phenomenon seemed to be transcendental both in technological and on mental levels. In other words, UFO behavior and intentions were too confusing even for the military.

Polish pilots who decided to share their UFO stories with ufologists probably had never met with any problems of an official nature though most of them decided to go on the record after retirement. As it was said before, most of the reported sightings were from the pre-1989 period. We do not know what was going on among the powers-that-be with regards to UFO related incidents during this era in Polish history. Although for the Air Force the UFO problem had always been deemed as *taboo and* after 1989 it became even and *greater taboo.*

"Mentioning UFOs in our official documentation would be taken as accepting the existence of unidentified flying objects of extraterrestrial origin, not only in the Polish Army but also the of the whole Warsaw Treaty. Instructions in the Warsaw pact were unified. But it was not forbidden to gather reports on strange occurrences in the airspace. I dealt with it and hoped it would be continued" – said Grundman. *"In today's Polish Army no one is collecting*

UFO reports. Ufologists often mention that our Army is concealing UFO data but in fact it has no data at all! After my departure, systematic gathering of information about the phenomenon ceased."

Though Grundman seems sincere and straightforward, his statements are not taken at face value by Polish ufologists. Maybe the Polish Air Force is not gathering such reports systematically, as he said, but it is still obliged to explain strange things which take place in the airspace over Poland. And as my work has shown, every year brings yet more and more spectacular incidents.

There is no doubt that the Polish Army has kept its eye on ufologists in the past and is still doing so even today. There were several possible attempts of military-induced disinformation on the UFO field In Poland and I too may have been a victim of this myself (you can find details in the chapter on UFO crashes in Poland). But let us instead now proceed to the best and most controversial UFO experiences of Polish military personnel. From the large catalogue of known UFO cases (collected, amongst others, by Leśniakiewicz and Rzepecki), I have chosen cases involving group pilot sightings and attempts to shoot down UFOs by Polish military aircraft.

Examples of military sightings

From 1958, a year of intensified UFO activity over Poland comes an interesting report of three separate encounters from pilot, Mr. Leszczyński, of unexplained aerial phenomenon over Poznań. On September 29th, during a training flight, he was overtaken by strange, bright, spherical object. The same appeared during his next mission and on that occasion he decided to approach it. But after several minutes the UFO was gone. On September 30th, during a night flight with a student pilot, Leszczyński saw two big *circles of light* with another pair some 12 miles away. According to his report, he managed to make a close approach during which one of the objects shot off while the other grew dimmer though its *dark silhouette* could still be seen in the in the sky. After a short while this dark object began to move away which apparently caused the student pilot a great deal of concern.

Gen. Apoloniusz Czernów (born in 1929) – was a man who had a long and prosperous career in the military, diplomacy and ministerial, and is probably the highest ranking Polish official who shared his UFO experience and also revealed an amount of other very controversial information. For example, he went on the record stating that he was informed of two mysterious cases of Polish Air Force jets that allegedly disappeared while trying to intercept a UFO.

His own personal UFO sighting took place in August 1958.

"As an assistant to the commander of the 3rd Fighter Regiment in Wrocław, I was, like every other pilot in the regiment on call. In those days we were often send to intercept balloons released from the München area (Munich in Germany). On the day in question I took off and then flew into the Jelenia Góra – Zgorzelec – Świdnica area to intercept a balloon. I did not succeed because it flew past me over into Czechoslovakian airspace. So I was returning back to base somewhat disappointed as every pilot looked upon the downing of object in the air as a kind of adventure. I was flying at 26 thousand feet. It was midday. Clouds were sparse, only a few cumulus. When I reached Świdnica, I saw an object over the clouds. I took it for another balloon. I reported it to the command who gave me permission intercept it providing I had enough fuel. I turned my Lim-5 [MiG-17] toward the balloon. I assumed that it must be approximately 9 miles away and at a height 3200 feet.

But when I got close to the alleged balloon, its shape and color surprised me. It was a cigar turned at an angle of 45 degrees to the horizontal level, silvery-orange in color and pulsating with a weird light. Confused, I took it for a new kind of balloon. I contacted the command, asking for permission to shoot. When I approached the object, something strange happened. The target began to ascend with a speed far exceeding my airplane's capabilities. It began heading north. When I reached 47.5 thousands feet, the object changed color to orange-red and in several seconds just took off. Back at the base I was informed that our radar detected nothing. I was also informed that another other pilot from Krzesiny AFB also tried to intercept something similar in the Wolsztyn area but to no avail."

In July of 1983 a similar scenario involving Cpt. Praszczałek took place over Darłowo airfield where an unauthorized object appeared. According to reports, it was a rotating, oblong object with a steel-colored covering. When the pilot tried to shoot it down, it stopped and changed position rapidly. When Praszczałek's put his finger on the trigger during a second attempt to shoot it down, the UFO repeated the earlier maneuver.

The event was corroborated by Col. Marek Jucewicz:

"An alarm was called on the 7th of July. We were ordered to intercept an object that was seen on radar screens. While returning from above the sea to Darłowo area, I saw a dark-brown, metallic cylinder. It was flying at 11 thousand feet. We approached and got within 220 yards. I saw it very well. The object had no windows, door, hatches or engines. It consisted of a solid hull, 50 feet long and 6 feet across, rotating around its axis. After reporting the

details, we were ordered to shoot it down. When my colleague prepared the gun, the object suddenly shot up! It went too high to about 30 thousand feet. We returned back to base where an official interrogation followed…"

Grundman reported that in the autumn of 1983 a cigar-shaped UFO had been tracked by two helicopters and a fighter jet. During an incident over Powidz airfield, the appearance of a luminous *cigar* caused a blackout and communication chaos. The same object had apparently previously been chased by helicopters in Łęczyca.

One of the most intriguing cases comes from Damian Trela's archive. The witness (who requested anonymity), now living in Oborniki Śląskie (śląskie), said that it took place in 1968 or 1969 over the Modlin area. At about 9 pm the witness took off in a MiG-21 for a short, routine mission. Initially this problem free flight turned into something quite different when he saw two objects approaching from the left side of his aircraft.

"He saw two disc-shaped objects moving at the same level and the same speed as his MiG. At a certain moment both approached to very dangerously close distance of about 30-50 feet. Both objects looked identical and were white in color. Both objects emitted a bright but non dazzling light. Each was of about 6-10 feet in diameter" – Damian wrote.

"The main witness immediately contacted his partner (in another MiG) who stated that he too could see identical objects on his right hand side. Both pilots were not able to explain this sighting any conventional way. They wondered if they had observed some kind of secret NATO objects. During the sighting their contact with their controller was lost and then also contact between the two pilots began to deteriorate as well. Four unidentified objects followed the two MiGs for another 3-6 miles, then accelerated and overtook them disappearing into the distance. The whole sighting lasted about 5 minutes and during that time the objects remained invisible to onboard radar. For a while the witnesses thought about attacking the objects but the discs were far too close. After the mission both the pilots were asked to explain the communication problems."

A similar case but involving 7 airplanes from the Mierzęcice base, according to Grundman, took place in 1980:

"During interception exercises, 7 MiG-12s noticed that an object similar a saucer, pulsating alternately with lights, approached them. It had a blue-gray cupola on top and was three-times bigger than any of the aircraft. It flew to each of the MiG's making maneuvers around them and seemingly breaking laws physics. The training exercise was changed and now the mission was to try and shoot down the UFO as soon as possible" – he said.

During nights of April 22nd to 23rd 1982, another group of pilots observed a UFO during a night mission in the northwestern area of Poland, in an area from Elbląg to Olsztyn and Ostróda. Reports of this event gathered by researcher, Andrzej Remlein, included the independent accounts of four military pilots of which A.P. was the most experienced one. In the description below he shares details of a very untypical unidentified object, incomparable to many other UFO sightings of a similar type.

"I was at 47.5 thousand feet when in the distance, somewhere over Morąg or Zalewo, I saw a weird light. Then I heard my colleagues speaking in the radio: 'Look right. What's that strange light?' I realised that they saw it too but I was in the closest proximity. It did not appear on the radar. It was something odd but also unique. From this distance it looked like a cloud with the central part raised up and some hazy sides. It was emanating a strong light and then I noticed that it was emanating beams of light from its underside. When I was about 1.8-2.5 miles away, I saw it very clearly, realising that it was UFO. The central part was a cupola made as if of a condensed, white light. Around it you could see the some sort of vapor, something similar to gas or smoke. When I got closer, I realised that the main object was not solid at all. Light beams sent down from this phenomenon were also very clear but ended somewhere in the mid air" – A.P. reported, adding that witnesses on the ground would not be able to differentiate this giant object from that of a large star.

The reports above seem to corroborate what I had already previously mentioned. Despite many attempts, the Air Force in Poland (as in other countries) seemed ineffective in dealing with the UFO phenomenon. These objects seemed too advanced and in some way anticipated human decisions. Regardless of its origin, fortunately they were not openly hostile.

Other personnel's sightings

During his service in the Air Force, my father gained access to a number of confidential reports including different information that required a cover up or some modification at least before being made public. Occasionally these reports involved pilots' encounters with *luminous spheres*. My father was unfortunately not very interested in them but he did confirm that such UFO reports were not rare and that they had a considerable amount of them. But UFO sightings in the People's Polish Army were not limited to on duty pilots and included supporting personnel or even airfield guards.

In 2008 I was contacted by Mr. K. W. who in February 1984 had commanded a group of soldiers of the 103rd Regiment directed to guard warehouses at Przasnysz airfield. On that day, just before the end of *Dziennik* (*Daily TV News*) which was compulsory viewing for every soldier, he went outside with his assistant to look into the pitch black sky covered with clouds. The weather was calm, cold and windless. Suddenly they both noticed a light coming in their direction.

"We assumed that it was at a maximum height of 150 feet above the ground but we could not make out more than an outline of some oval object which behind it was scattered with light." -he said. *"Seeing the objects contour, we realised it was huge. It was moving soundlessly and when it came directly over us, we could feel some sort of paralysis. We tried to seek cover but the terror was too strong and we remained rooted to the spot. When the object passed over, we noticed a kind of a big lamp with a black stain inside located on its rear part. Then we noticed two smaller ones – to the right and above. It looked as if the object was propelled by that light. Although I was very frightened, I decided to take a Kalashnikov Automate (in Polish Army known as AK) and shoot at that reflector or light. But immediately I received a mental communication: 'DO NOT TOUCH OR YOU WILL BE PARALYZED'. I was terrified and unable to move. I wanted it to depart as soon as possible"* – the man reported.

Lt. K.W. added that the object was about 70-100 feet across and completely silent. When the UFO disappeared, he called the flight controller to ask about air traffic in the Przasnysz area. "Nothing is in air" – he was informed.

The Przasnysz encounter may be to some researchers the best evidence for the very mysterious characteristics of UFOs encountered by military witnesses. Although these objects were of a technical nature, they also seemed to be able to interfere with human consciousness, reacting when threatened by an attack. It fulfills Jacques Vallée's remark that during close encounters, it is always the UFO that is in control and not the human observers.

Details illustrating the official protocol of flight controllers to incidents with unidentified targets came from Mr. Kazimierz Lubertowicz's – former chief of air traffic control at the Mielec airfield (podkarpackie) report. Mielec owns the Polish Aviation Works (PZL) – the largest aerospace manufacturer in post-war Poland but objects encountered over the area had nothing in common with and of his company's products. According to Lubertowicz and his co-workers with whom Arek Miazga contacted, the Mielec area used to be the location of numerous

UFO encounters. One of the most interesting, also including Lubertowicz, will be presented in the next chapter on mass UFO sightings.

But let's skip to the incident during summer night exercises from 1984 or 1985.

"I'm sure that the incident I will mention has been reported to both military and civilian authorities. The most intense activity of those objects over Mielec and in the eastern part of the country was a period from 1971 to 1994.

During nighttime flights over the airfield and in a 25 miles range, on a certain evening, maybe about 8 pm, in autumn or late summer, I received details from the pilot that something was approaching from the south-west. In such conditions every aircraft must display the correct lighting but the object in question did not and was instead a red-orange dot. We assumed it must be located several miles away from Mielec. It remained motionless but too big to be Venus. Lacking any reports of aircraft activities in Mielec, I called the Military Service of Air Traffic in Sandomierz, then Radiotechnic Battalion in Warsaw, a number of airports and Air Force Command but all excluded the possibility of conventional aircraft being present in the area. Soon the appropriate services requested more information. The pilot did not approach but kept eye on the object from a distance. The phenomenon had been witnessed for about 2 hours by 30-40 people including airfield workers and military personnel. Also Mielec Aeroclub pilots witnessed it. The object in question was floating away very slowly in Rzeszów direction. When the pilot I spoke to (Jan O.) flew over the forests between Mielec, Kolbuszowa and Nowa Dęba, he reported another piece of information. I estimate that the object was flying at a level of 1300-1600 feet" – Lubertowicz reported.

Another interesting report came from a helicopter pilot and a mechanic who late at night, on April 21st 1979, were returning to their unit. In the Błonie area, the pair traveling by car saw an object descending rapidly over the road. Thinking it was an attempt to emergency landing, they immediately arranged their car in such a way as to try and show solid ground to their fellow pilot in trouble. But then the object unveiled its real nature.

"After a while it became clear that it could not be a helicopter or any other conventional craft. The object consisted of four large lights. Though nothing could be seen in the space between them, we assumed that it must be a solid flying object. At first we tried to listen for its engine sounds but we heard

nothing! It looked to me to be more that 100 feet in length. The object stopped and hovered for a while about 300 feet above the ground and then shot up without any acceleration phase" – the witness reported.

Civilian pilots' encounters

Reports of Polish civil/amateur pilots' UFO encounters remain scarce but the passion, interest and tradition of private flying in Poland remains very strong and still remains widespread across the country. While the Air Force is a hermetic, elite circle, there are many flying clubs all over the country although only a small percent of people can afford to purchase their own ultra-light machines.

Stories of UFO sightings circulate in both the civilian and amateur pilot communities but only in rare instances have made their way to the outside world. An encounter with a spectacular object happened to Sławomir L. who on May 16th 1980, took off with his glider (*Pirat* type) from Rudniki airfield near Częstochowa. On his flight path to Działoszyn (łódzkie) the pilot fought with tricky weather conditions. Reaching the cement mill in Działoszyn at about 3 pm, out of the corner of his eye he noticed an object maneuvering across the fumes from factory chimneys below. Seconds later the UFO appeared in front of the glider. Sławomir R. turned sideways and tried decrease speed, catching a glimpse of the object. It was in the shape of an isosceles triangle (with side length about 30 feet) a dull color, something between brown and deep-green. It seemed uniform, with no typical craft features or markings. During his sighting the pilot noticed that the triangle turned up one of its corners at an angle of 45 degrees in an apparent attempt to correct its flight. Then it changed its orientation to horizontal, momentarily shrank in size and then disappeared! Rzepecki who examined the case mentioned that a very similar object had been witnessed on the same day by man from Wieluń area.

After the NATO accession in 1999, pilots' UFO reports ceased to flow. Is the Polish Air Force who operates at NATO borders with Russia still recognising that the best way to deal publicly with UFOs is to keep silent and disregard the problem? There is one good reason to continue that practice (but with no connection to cover-up of extraterrestrial presence). If the UFO problem gained official acceptance as unidentified activity, the Air Force would be forced by public opinion to react and check every single sighting. But they do not have the time or the money for any such undertaking. It's as simple as that. More importantly, over the last few decades it became apparent that these objects are not openly hostile. So involuntarily the Polish Air Force must share the skies with an anomaly with still unidentified objectives.

QUOTATIONS SOURCES

Piotr Cielebiaś and Michał Kuśnierz Archives / infra.org.pl

Damian Trela Archives

Blania-Bolnar Z., *Obecność UFO*, V. 1, Warszawa 1988.

Domański J., *Zagadka epoki*, Warszawa 1979.

Harpula W., *Polskie wojsko na tropie UFO* – wywiad z płk R. Grundmanem, Onet.pl, 22/06/2009.

Miazga A., *UFO nad Podkarpaciem*, Ropczyce 2013 (ebook).

Rzepecki B., *Bliskie spotkania z UFO w Polsce*, Tarnów 1995.

Rzepecki B., Grundman R., *Polscy piloci i UFO*, Kraków 1999 (special issue of *Czas UFO* magazine).

Chapter 10

MASS SIGHTINGS & GREAT FLYBYS

Transforming UFO witnessed by hundreds? • Exotic aerial vessel over marshlands • Rzeszów stationary sphere • Pilot sent to investigate "a thing" 3-hour-long triangle sighting

SKEPTICS often stress that UFO stories remain suspicious because unidentified objects tend to manifest themselves only in isolated areas and appear to completely unprepared witnesses. They are partially right but it is a presumption growing from lack of understanding. Elusiveness and the seeming absurdity seem to be inbuilt features of the UFO phenomenon. But please do not misunderstand this. Most people confronted with the UFO enigma tend to interpret it through their own priori assumption concerning extraterrestrial visitors in their magical flying machines. That interpretation compared with the reality of phenomenon can often produce a mental conflict. But throughout the 70 years of official recognition of the UFO enigma we have gathered enough reliable data in order to make comparative analyses. They unveil a perceptible pattern in UFOs behavior including their external lack of logic and interest in official contact as well as the ability to manipulate witness' consciousness. That is the real, still inexplicable nature of the phenomenon, very exotic to our way of thinking and mentality to say the least.

Amongst attention-grabbing UFO encounters in Poland were also those witnessed by groups of observers scattered over large areas. Incidents of that kind remained characteristic for the PRP period and can be reconstructed based largely on local media coverage. Some of these sightings even elicited an official response. The following reports refer to phenomena that cannot be explained in astronomical or technical (man-made) terms and demonstrate that UFO encounters are not simply observed by lone individuals in isolated areas.

Mass sighting – mass confusion

An uncanny mass UFO sighting over a multiregional geographical area took place on August 20th 1979. Piechota and Rzepecki estimated that around 119 people witnessed the strange things in the air on that evening. These reports mentioned several types of UFOs: cylindrical, cylindrical dividing into luminous spheres, those spheres themselves or cylindrical flying in the company of spheres. The most controversial aspect is connected with the sighting localisation. It embraced vast areas of the northern and eastern part of the country, including the main cities of Sopot, Gdańsk, Olsztyn, and even Warszawa. Numerous reports of those events appeared in *Dziennik Bałtycki* and *Kurier Polski* (local press). The first official explanation of Dr. Henryk Kuźmiński assumed that the reports were induced by a kind of cosmic body burning up on re-entering the atmosphere. That was supposed to explain the reports of the strange cylindrical object that divided in two or emitted luminous balls of light. But according to the eyewitnesses from the Gdańsk Bay area, this hypothesis simply was not able to explain everything.

Lawyer Mieczysław Mertz who was vacationing in Sopot stated that the object he saw *"resembled a cigar ejecting a smoky trail and flames with a row of square windows along its surface"*. Another vacationer, Jerzy Lebiedziński, saw the same cigar in Jurata: "Its luminosity intensified above the coast and the object split into two pieces. The second element, also very luminous, departed in the direction of Gdańsk." Other reports mentioned the intense brilliance of the object, multi-colored bands or lights on its surface and the total lack of any sound. Henryk Jeruzal's letter to *Głos Wybrzeża* (*Voice of the Coast*) informed its readers that he had been observing the spectacle from Pruszcz Gdański and had observed an oblong object that then transformed itself into a *ball*. Bogdan Śmiech from Malbork (in close vicinity to the south-west of Pruszcz) saw only *"9 or 10 intensely bright balls of light, 3-4 miles above the ground"*.

The first reports of the *cigar-shaped object* from Gdańsk Bay came from around 8:30 pm. But shortly after 7:30 pm, in the Bydgoszcz area (south of Gdańsk) apparently the same object had appeared, coming from the north-western. On that occasion *the cigar with windows* remained at a low altitude and produced a number of confusing reports. Adam S. – one of the first witnesses from the State Agricultural Farm in Jastrzębie, noted: *"It was at first high in the air but it could be clearly seen that it was descending. At first I took it for a malfunctioning aircraft because a long smoke trail followed the object."*

More shocking details were provided by the B.s (real name withheld) from Świecie and Wisła. The main witness along with his wife decided to perform some ornithological studies on the marsh between the Dziki and Ernestowo villages.

According to his account, some weird object stopped for a while over the Ernestowo village, only 1300 ft in the air providing him with the ideal situation to examine it with binoculars.

"I'm not a fearful man but the thing I saw was literally impossible. I have seen many things but how tons of steel could hover in the mid-air without making a noise? I examined it closely with my binoculars but saw no element that could form an opening to the object. But five large, square and evenly placed windows were clearly visible on its surface. Three of them emanated with orange light but of less intensity in comparison to the front part of the object. Two other windows remained obscured" – he reported.

To sum this up, the pair saw (with binoculars but also with the naked eye) an oblong object resembling a metallic wagon with a kind of *engine compartment* at the rear part and an intensely orange-colored front segment. What is interesting is that he also noticed, quite bizarrely, a 30 foot long propeller and stabilisers at the rear part of the craft (!). His account could be disputed but Mr. B. was an experienced soldier claiming that the sighting *"stirred strong emotions within"*. After more than 30 seconds, the object evidently started its engines since witnesses observed a gush of sparks. It then departed with amazing speed, breaking all known laws of physics, mechanics and aerodynamics…

The events from August 20th remained a mystery. Although many witnesses gave similar descriptions of the oblong craft, other details varied. Could it be explained by the fact that the structure of the object disintegrated in the atmosphere? An astronomical interpretation became the official accepted one though the local press undermined it and did not necessarily agree. The truth is possibly hidden between the hypothesis of some non-identified rocket disintegration (that could look similar to the sequence of events form August 20th) and Mr. B.'s report describing an exotic unidentified object even in ufological terms.

A nearly identical sequence of events took place on November 5th 1990 in a large part of Southern Poland. Witnesses again described a cigar-shaped object accompanied with spherical objects but also some cupola-shaped UFOs. *Kurier Zachodni (Western Courier)* reported: *"In the Opole district hundreds of people witnessed the phenomenon. Corporals Arkadiusz Adamiec, Tadeusz Krzyżak and Mariusz Skaźnik from the military unit on Domański Street in Opole, said in unison: 'We saw a group of balls quickly flying towards the center of Opole. Most of these objects emitted long, bright trails – something like a firework. There were about 15-20 of them in total. After a few seconds another group passed overhead but these were not as large as the previous ones."* Paweł Woźniak, who saw the phenomenon from the opposite part of Opole, reported: *"It was not a rocket, firework or a jet. I could identify the latter with engine sounds. I also excluded a meteor…"* Witnesses from the Kielce area, 125 miles to the west, described the object as evidently cigar shaped. Official reorganisation was similar to that from August 20th 1979: it was just a group of meteorites.

Podkarpacie mass event

On July 13th 1984 a mysterious object came into view above Rzeszów. It appeared at about 4:30 pm and for a long time just remained stationary in the air. According to reports in the *Nowiny (News)* newspaper the light ball then began slowly floating away. Janusz Szpont – flight controller from Jasionka airfield said it could be at 6500 feet level and headed towards Mielec where the most interesting part of the sighting soon occurred. It involved Mr. Lubertowicz who was informed by the respective weather services that no meteorological balloons had been released in the area. Whatever it was this object must be something different. It was therefore decided to limit air traffic over area. The decision was made to send an Iskra jet trainer on a scout mission. After consultations with Lubertowicz, the plane piloted by Henryk Bronowicki took off.

"When I arrived at the airfield many workers had their eyes fixed to the sky" – he said in interview with Arek Miazga.

"When I got out of my car and looked up, I saw a strange, silvery ball of large size, hovering motionlessly in the air. On that day I got a scheduled flight to Nisko, Leżajsk and Rzeszów. When the mission was over, Kazimierz Lubertowicz – the air traffic director, after checking my fuel level, asked me to approach that object. During the flight the radar station in Sandomierz tracked Iskra but not the strange sphere. Getting closer I observed that it was not a meteorological balloon.

I was at 24,600 feet and we were not equipped with oxygen masks. The object was moving away and that was strange. After some time we gave up the chase and leveled off. The object also changed its altitude so we decide to approach it one more time but all in vain once again. The object retreated again and I could not close on it."

Bronowicki was forced to land due to an approaching storm. He remembered that the ground crew was still dumbfounded with the UFO hovering motionlessly despite the strong wind. Bronowicki had been previously interviewed by the press and his report appeared in the *Nowiny newspaper*. He stated that the alleged *balloon* was about 80 feet in diameter and its surface had a metallic coating reflecting the sunlight. Some dark points looked as if they were strapped to its bottom section.

Głos Załogi (*The Crew's Voice*) newspaper mentioned other sightings of the same object in the Mielec area. Some described it as *transparent ball*. But before the Rzeszów manifestation, the same UFO had been observed over Przemyśl.

"On July 13th Andrzej W. – a worker at the Customs Office and Andrzej S. from the Regional Prosecutor's Office, both from Przemyśl, at about 4:05 pm noticed a strange object over the Pstrowski estate. Something similar to disc or sphere floated directly over them. The sky was misty and the object emitted a light weaker than those of the sun but almost white in color. It remained stationary for about 3 minutes and then disappeared without a trace" – Kurier Polski (The Polish Courier) reported.

The press soon announced that the mystery was over after a man from Tarnów found the debris of a metrological probe hanging from a tree. Other hypotheses also embraced the probe possibility but for spying purposes rather than meteorological. But both Bronowicki and Lubertowicz's group comments casts serious doubts on that possibility.

Zamość triangle

Zamość is called the *Padua of the north* thanks to its unique architecture that fortunately survived all of the historical turmoil Poland has experienced. It is a city of unique style, culture and history that made it a *pearl of the renaissance*. On September 18th 1982 numerous inhabitants of the city region were witness to a 3-hour-long sighting of a stationary, triangular object. Despite the controversies invoked by the incident, it did not draw mass public attention (maybe due to intensified press surveillance in the Martial Law period).

"Residents of the Suchowola village saw it for the first time at about 3pm. Mrs. Katarzyna Kudełko, a local inhabitant, began observing it with binoculars. She said: 'That objects shape was close to an isosceles triangle. The top that pointed southward possessed a strong, metallic (?) light. Two other tips (forming its base) displayed two pulsating lights that changed colors but much weaker in brightness than the previous one'. " – Sztandar Ludu (People's Banner) reported.

The newspaper report mentioned that further reports were consistent with that of Mrs. Kudelko. But before too long the *Kurier Lubelski* (*Lublin Courier*) published a semi-official *explanation* from Jerzy Rachwał – the director of the local flying club in which in his opinion the object was… an *"artificial satellite of oblong shape, with antennas which were visible when viewed with binoculars"*. Rachwał also stated that the object was not stationary but moved slowly. His theory was so opposite to the local resident's reports that he was boldly criticised by a reader in his letter to

Kurier Lubelski:

"I am amused with the theories of the quoted Mr. Rachwał. I can not believe that a pilot could say something like that. I rather suppose that it is an attempt to calm the public with a pseudo-scientific theory" – he wrote, explaining why it could not be a satellite.

Other possible mass UFO sightings involved also a number of false alarms. This was the Częstochowa sighting from early the 1990's when a bright spot seemingly hovering over the world-famous sanctuary in Jasna Góra triggered rumors and speculations. It turned to be nothing more than the planet Venus.

It turns out that the controversial elements of UFO encounters are proportional to the number of witnesses. In other words, mass sightings pose more problems and questions than typical UFO incidents. The cases in this chapter are such examples and despite their scale and potential they remain literally forgotten.

Those officials who were concerned that such UFO the reports would not induce unnecessary concern in Polish society accomplished their task. Cases of Polish multi-UFO *flybys* are now completely neglected and unknown to younger generations interested in ufology, let alone enthusiasts abroad outside of our nation.

Quotations sources

Piotr Cielebiaś and Michał Kuśnierz Archives / infra.org.pl

Arek Miazga Archives / Arekmiazga.blogspot.com

Jerzy Marcinek Archives

Miazga A., *UFO nad Podkarpaciem*, Vol. 1, Ropczyce 2013 (ebook).

Rzepecki B., *Bliskie spotkania z UFO w Polsce*, Tarnów 1995.

Piechota K., Rzepecki B., *UFO nad Polską*, Białystok 1996.

UFO nad Zamościem, Sztandar Ludu, 21/09/1982.

Kto wyjaśni zamojską zagadkę?, Kurier Lubelski, 10/10/1982.

UFO w Przemyślu, Kurier Polski, 04-06/08/1984.

Balon czy nieznane zjawisko?, Nowiny, 27/07/1984.

Chapter 11

THE BĘDZIENICA-NOCKOWA INCIDENT

Farmhouse flooded by light • Red pyramid in the field • Barn on fire
"Dad, Green men approach us!" • Beings with angular faces
High strangeness case or taboo?

AREK Miazga (born 1976) is a very stubborn researcher. When the precursors of Polish ufology announced in 2005 that all is over, the UFO subject is non-traversable and it was time to close the *UFO* magazine, Arek didn't give up. His persistence resulted in the publication of *UFO over Podkarpacie* – a book listing the most unusual, interesting and controversial reports from his region covering an area slightly bigger than Connecticut in the USA. Unidentified objects activity over Podkarpacie (literally Sub-Carpathian) is so high that it used to be called the *UFO pole (UFO hot-spot)*.

Arek lives in Ropczyce near Rzeszów – the regions capital and simultaneously the *Polish UFO center* with the highest amount of sightings amongst all of Poland's large cities. Rzeszów has even got its own *anomalous zones* where unknown activity seems to concentrate. But in this chapter we want to discuss one of the most interesting CE-3 files from Arek's archive. The Będzienica-Nockowa encounter started with the sighting of some weird lights over fields in a remote village and finished with a farming family's encounter with bizarre humanoids peering out from a *luminous screen*.

UFO on a warm night

Arek Miazga became aware of Mr. Kazimierz S.'s family experience from their friend and he did not waste any time before he visited the main witness. The whole sequence from that summer evening in 1988 was well remembered by Mr. Kazimierz, his wife and two daughters. At the time of the encounter they all lived in Będzienica village located 15 miles away from Ropczyce. The event in question took place in late July, "just before harvest time" – the family claimed. On that warm evening, at about 9pm., Mr. Kazimierz, his wife and a daughter were on their way home in their horse-drawn cart from the local brick manufacturer where they all worked. Nearing a curve by their house Mrs. Zofia noticed a light in the sky and she mentioned this to her husband. It was a red-colored object in the shape of a sphere. It looked just like the UFO from Mr. Machowski's photo in Wicie. Whatever it was, it was high up in the air and soon was obscured by the buildings of their farm.

The family reached home in a little while and began their nighttime duties. It was getting dark when the first of a strange series of events began. In Mr. Kazimierz's words, unexpectedly the whole area was flooded with a bright light. *"One would at night find a lost needle in that glare"* – he related. Soon all the family members (involving also Mrs. Zofia's mother) rushed outside and saw a number of spherical objects hovering over nearby fields. There were two groups with three white lights in horizontal rows, one positioned close to the other. At first Mr. Kazimierz took the lights for harvesters or tractors but they were stationary and soundless. Intrigued, he decided to alarm his neighbor. Soon both found themselves on the road from where the family had seen the red object at 9pm. Admiring this strange spectacle, soon the neighbor could see even stranger things in the distance.

> *"It was an enormous red-orange triangle located around 1.8 miles in a northeastern direction. Mr. Kazimierz said that it seemed non-solid but made of fire or light. This object was taller than the neighboring pine trees and its luminosity was not very intense. Moreover, it seemed to go up and down alternately. After 5 minutes the triangle suddenly disappeared. But the most intriguing fact was that it emanated some very odd sounds. 'I had never heard anything like that before'* – *the witness mentioned. In his opinion, it was similar to a 'honk' but high-pitched"* – Arek Miazga wrote.

After several moments of confusion, the two men continued to ponder the nature and origin of these spheres. Instantly, another sighting was added to the chain of events. Mr. Kazimierz noted that another neighbor's barn burst in flames! Without deliberation on possible causes and connections with the UFO activity, the man rushed home, started his motorcycle and headed in that direction to try and help if at all possible. He also took his two daughters (respectively 16 and 14-year-old) who were as curious as their father.

Driving along dusty lanes through the artificially illuminated landscape, they reached the neighboring farm in no time. But upon arriving, the father and daughters noticed no fire… At that moment Mr. Kazimierz felt a bit uncomfortable. His neighbor's family seemingly hadn't been aware of the UFO's presence. The now slightly frightened witness understood that he was dealing with something out of the ordinary. Overcoming his fears, he decided to drive to a nearby hill in order to catch the last glimpse of the brilliant spheres before they were gone forever.

"Look, Green people approach!"

The witness and his daughters soon stood on a hill admiring the landscape with the two groups of unidentified objects in the distance. Soon they noticed another row of lights positioned low over the fields in northerly direction, previously obscured by some hills. Mr. Kazimierz then realised that it was the beams of light that had been cast into the direction of the barn causing to look like it was on fire.

"Beams of light emanated from each object and they widened and spread out in the distance. The witness compared them to a torch light but not so diffused. Mr. Kazimierz focused his attention on the northern group of lights, while his daughters had been observing the southern ones. Unexpectedly he heard one of the girl's scream: 'Oh my Good! Dad, look! Green people approach from the direction of Rzeszów!" – Arek wrote.

The witness detailed the encounter in the following words:

"One daughter screamed (I can't remember which one), grasping my shirt: 'Dad! Green people! Over there, coming from Rzeszów's direction!' I turned back but saw nothing. But when they pointed me in the direction of the object, shrieking with fear, I could see them. It was a kind of screen, but huge one, maybe 10 feet in height. One man, a gigantic one, stood there… It was all white and hovering maybe 60-100 feet over the ground. It was clearly visible, with dark contours. I jumped on my bike and started the engine!" – he said.

Mr. Kazimierz noticed some problems with the clutch of his motorcycle but was still managed to drive away. In his opinion, the UFO was approaching him side on. At some moment he made a sharp turn to the left and lost the object from sight. In the meantime he realised that there was another, smaller being in the rectangular screen.

Mrs. Barbara – one of the man's daughters, reported more astonishing details.

"It was brilliant, especially when approaching us" – she said.

"The figures had angular heads, resembling some geometric figures… They looked like armored people. They had big, clumsy palms and disproportional arms reaching to their knees."

Her story turned to be slightly different than that of her father. This situation might stem from the fact that she could observe it for longer than Mr. Kazimierz who quickly decided to take his daughters to a safer place. Mrs. Barbara agreed that at some point two beings appeared inside the screen but in fact it wasn't strictly rectangular. That two-dimensional object was morphing from circle (at first) to triangle and rectangle. In the progress the beings changed positions and even at some point she counted four green figures in total. In her opinion, they seemed humanoid in shape and their coating or outfit was deep-greenish color and made of a rough-looking texture. Their geometrical heads, without facial details, gave them a very bizarre appearance. Throughout the encounter the beings remained stationary and faced witnesses.

When all three drove down the hill, Mr. Kazimierz said that the fear left him so he could smoothly continue his way home which was illuminated by the lights from the spherical objects. But just some 300 feet from their farm, another strange object appeared in the sky. Along with daughters he saw a *tailed ball* of *fire* descending very rapidly and disappearing in the area where the triangle had been previously been seen. It was their last shared sighting. Soon the girls, tired and frightened, went asleep. So did Mrs. Zofia but her husband was still observing the two groups of spherical objects from the bedroom windows upstairs. According to him, at about 4 am they quickly rearranged into a more complex group involving 7 objects (from original 6) and remained in that configuration for another hour when Mr. S. decided go to go to sleep.

The main witness said that on the next day he felt unwell and finally he had to be taken to hospital. Not surprisingly the sighting left many unanswered questions. The first one involved other potential eyewitnesses. It was without question that someone must have seen the luminous objects. Mr. Kazimierz soon met a man from a neighboring village who also saw weird lights over the fields. Local gossip led to a rumor that there was a bus driver who encountered the UFOs but most of the local residents made no reports of the red triangular object or the spheres.

Arek Miazga is sure that the family of Mr. Kazimierz told him a genuine story. But the real nature of their brush with the unknown remains a mystery. Could it be that it involved deep consciousness-related effects? The presence of other independent witness may suggest that some kind of rural *taboo* mechanism was at work. Hardworking farmers might have no time to pay attention to lights in the fields which they would assume were simply other harvesters hard at work. Perhaps there were other witnesses after all?

QUOTATIONS SOURCES

Arek Miazga Archives / Arekmiazga.blogspot.com.

Miazga A., UFO nad Podkarpaciem, Vol. 1, Ropczyce 2013.

Miazga A., Bliskie spotkanie w Będzienicy-Nockowej, infra.org.pl.

Chapter 12

DECADE OF CONTROVERSIES – CASES FROM THE 1990's

Spacemen sightings in Brzózka • Miniature UFO • Saucers the of 90's
Adventure on the road to Opole • St. Ann's Hill "ufological shock"
UFO over military range

IN 1989 the political system in Poland changed during a peaceful revolution and capitalism replaced the old economical structure. You probably heard stories about Lech Wałęsa – an electrician who became president but the historical truth behind that process is more complicated. Initiated evolution caused the quick westernisation of Poland but the costs of transformation were very high. Polish industry had been ruined down in 1990s which resulted in a high unemployment rate and high social dissatisfaction. Contemporary Polish political elites form a *closed cast* separated from real problems of its citizens. So don't be surprised when someday you'll see in TV news mass protests in Poland similar to those which began the downfall of the Eastern Block.

But let us return to UFOs. The new decade brought another wave of sightings and changes in the ufological movement. In 1990 *UFO* quarterly (magazine) was issued for the very first time and so did *Nieznany Świat* (*World Unknown*). The latter, still in print today, is devoted to many aspects of the paranormal and fringe science. Its legendary editor, Marek Rymuszko – a well known journalist and lawyer, remains one of few in the subject who keeps up with high ethical and intellectual values. *Nieznany Świat* importance for ufology is strengthened by fact that during its 25 years of existence its editors compiled their own *X-files* from readers' reports and letters detailing strange experiences and encounters.

Despite the evident decrease in the number of reported cases, UFO sightings from the 1990's remained as complex and puzzling as those of previous decades although the most intriguing of these raised more questions than they provided answers to. Many were recollections of previous encounters.

The emergence of the bizarre Człuchów spacemen encounter from 1979 appeared in publication in the summer of 1990. Ryszard P. from Żabno (wielkopolskie) claimed that during a break in a long car voyage to Germany, he accidentally came across a group of *dwarf spacemen*. His unexpected confrontation with beings in puffy suits finished in a *missing time* episode.

Jumping spacemen and other miracles

Damian Trela during his stay in Wylatowo village where mysterious crop formations had been appearing for several summers (July) in row, found out about story of Ryszard P. from neighboring Żabno. The man claimed that on the 8th or 9th July 1990, while traveling by car to Germany, he made a stop in the Brzózka area to stretch his tired muscles. It was about 4 am when he left his car in the vicinity of the bridge on the Bóbr River and went for a short walk down a forest lane. Walking more than 30 yards into the trees, he could hear a peculiar sound which was unlike any typical wildlife noise. Trying to localise its source, he noticed a very large object. "*A bowl turned upside*" – he described its shape. A brilliant light was coming out of a wide opening in its lower part and from underneath the machine. Shocked Ryszard P. estimated that it must be 15 feet 10 inches across and about 80 feet tall. A nauseating odor he compared to *burned chocolate* permeated the area which, as it soon turned out, was under scrutiny of the bizarre crew of the *pot-like* machine.

> "*There were about 15 humanoids resembling mummies. They were about 4.5 feet tall, with conjoined legs and wearing a sort of deep-green uniform, tightly fitting their bodies. Their arms were very flexible and able to operate in various directions (as if devoid of elbows). He could see their fingers which resembled claws. Their faces were obscured with white plaques similar to welding masks or mirrors and their heads seemed set directly onto their torsos – puffy like stuffed bags*" – Damian wrote.

Ryszard P. stated the spacemen were engaged in *probing* or *research*. They poked plants with some oblong, pipe-like items, moving with *hops* like kangaroos. Unfortunately, at some point the witness involuntarily coughed and lost consciousness. He woke up in the same place an hour later but the craft and its bizarre occupants were nowhere to be seen. Confused, he found his car and drove away to the nearest border crossing. He could remember that awful smell and the taste of burned chocolate haunted him all day long.

Similar incidents always pose a number of questions, why do allegedly superiorly intelligent alien beings undertake the hazards of manned missions to Earth? If they are so far more technically advanced than us and prefer not to contact humans, they should surely use some sort of unmanned probes instead? It would be safer, cheaper and be less visible to the *subjects under observation* (i.e. us) would it not?

The sighting of something similar might have happened in the late 1990's to a local resident in Śrem during a stroll in the park:

"I'd just finished smoking a cigarette and trod the end under my foot. When I looked ahead, on the opposite side of the alley, I noticed a sphere floating in mid-air, slightly bigger than tennis ball. It was just a matter of seconds. When I caught a glimpse of the object it immediately floated away and disappeared.

Although the sighting was short, I could well remember its appearance. The ball was covered with irregular dots in pale hues of blue and green (it resembled military camouflage). A steel-colored, semi-circular notch ran from the upper to lower part. A similar one emerged from its right side stopped before intersecting the vertical one" – the witness remembered.

The problem of miniature UFOs is not confined to these few sightings. Arek Miazga reported a case involving group of children who during a wedding party in the 1980's. In that case, a little glowing sphere descended amongst the kids playing outside and then disappeared at a tremendous speed.

Silesian sightings: Cruising UFOs and deep shock

The last decade of the 20th century brought many cases to light in the Silesia macro-region in the south-western part of Poland. They included sightings in the Wrocław area and Opole region, with the St. Ann's Hill encounter as the most renowned one. In June 1997, over several consecutive nights, a group of young people had been observing the maneuvers of a number brilliantly illuminated objects. As a result, one of them almost went mad.

Before we proceed to that controversial encounter, it is worth noting that in the late 1990s there were several flying saucer sightings in various parts of the country. In 2013 we received the report of Mr. Patryk B. from Wrocław who claimed to have observed two objects of that type during a stroll in the park with his brother.

"It took place at the turn of June and July 1999" – he began his story.

"I was then 17 years old while my brother was just 15. I'm sure there must have been other witnesses as it took place during the daytime in a park lying between two large estates with tall apartment buildings. On the day in question, at about 11 or 12 am, we went for a stroll with our dog. I often took

my dog to the Western Park but on that day, due an injury to my leg (incurred during a recent parachute jump); I had to ask my brother for help in walking the dog. Sitting on a bench, I started to analyse the cloud cover, wondering if the weather would affect the s plans of my fellow parachutist colleagues. At some moment I saw a disc-shaped object passing over the trees and pointed it out to my brother. We had soon reached a small clearing but the object began to disappear behind the treetops. After a while I saw another, identical object. It was blue-gray in color with some light-blue squares on the bottom section."

According to the witness' sketch, the objects in question resembled giant plates with angular edges, each one with a row of blue lights on the bottom section. Both of the UFOs were heading in a north-eastern direction and were clearly below cloud level.

"The sighting impressed me so much that even today its recollection has made me excited. I had never seen anything like this before and surely it was not a plane, helicopter or balloon" – he said.

So amazed also were two other young men whose car in February 1998 was immobilised by huge object emitting a blinding light. JK and PZ were on their way from Opole to Niemodlin where they planned to meet up with friends. Suddenly the car radio off down and engine of their Fiat 125p (nicknamed *The Big One*) stalled. They found themselves in the middle of nowhere, in a cold and frosty darkness.

"It was only a matter of seconds. At the same time a very large object passed over us. We weren't able to recognise its shape because it was too dazzling. It was strange but we both looked up in unison. Luckily it was a straight section of road and we did not crash. We began shouting at one another because we were seriously frightened. I'd like to add that we weren't alcohol abusers and even today we are not what you would call timid" – the man, who is now a police officer, related.

"When the object passed over us and flew away, lights, radio and the engine just turned back on by themselves. We still had object in view. At first it ascended to 2500-3300 feet and accelerated in the direction of Niemodlin. We knew well the Opole area topography and realised that the UFO had descended somewhere over the road to Niemodlin, the exact place we were heading to. It prompted us to wonder if it would be waiting for us there."

The witnesses, both students at time of the encounter, fought off their fear and drove to a nearby hill to see if the object still could be seen in the distance.

"We stopped the car at the summit of the hill and saw the object again. It was

a spherical shape and emitted a dazzling light and hovered just over the top of the forest, 1-1.2 miles away. It remained stationary. 'Try to wink headlights in its direction' – I said to P. He rearranged the car, targeted the UFO and flashed the headlights several times. It was at this point that I became deadly frightened. The object started from its original position and approached us with enormous speed, flying 65-100 feet above the ground. I jumped into the car crying hysterically. P. also shouted and set off. About half a minute later we were already in the town center of Niemodlin."

Mr. JK tells us that he wondered if he should notify the Police but rejected the idea. In Poland the Police do not officially react to reports of UFO even it they might suggest a possible danger to national security. The same is with policemen encounter a UFO direct themselves. As you will see in one of following chapters, they are kindly persuaded by official principals to forget about what they have seen.

However, several months before the previous event in the St. Ann's Hill area – at a small local sanctuary occurred an encounter that was even mentioned on TV. Irrespective of the media fame it did not make the case any more reliable or clear. It must be said that the event took place under very some very *original* circumstances and resulted in a kind of *psychological disorder* to the main witness.

On Sunday, June 15th 1997, Grzegorz Nowak and his three friends left a disco party and set off to Opole – their hometown. At some point Nowak proposed to drive to St. Ann's Hill to admire the nighttime panoramic view. The eerie atmosphere of the place intrigued them so much that they returned there on several consequent nights. On Tuesday night Nowak claimed to observe some strange lights in the distance but the rest of the party took it be just ordinary lanterns. A sequence of high-strangeness events started on the next night when a group of five people noticed a number of lights making strange maneuvers and configurations over the fields at the foot of the hill. According to Janusz Zagórski who wrote about the case, Nowak and a friend decided to observe the lights from the vicinity of the St. Ann's Hill monument commemorating a battle waged there during the Silesian Uprising against the Germans in 1921. En route to the monument he saw an enormous screen moving over the area that ejected a luminous ball. In the meantime other witnesses tried to communicate with the dancing lights, giving signals with the car headlights. They also became very concerned about Nowak and his friend who had disappeared for about 2 hours and upon their return were completely unaware of this.

The fourth night brought forth the most terrific and controversial set of events. The four friends gathered at the same place waiting for UFOs that soon appeared. After again signaling with their car headlights they all witnessed the appearance of an enormous cigar-shaped craft, shooting out multicolored lights that hovered almost directly over them in the sky. Shortly thereafter a huge roaring sound was heard and all of the witnesses were of the opinion that a number of military aircraft had now also arrived in the area. When the aircraft had disappeared, the most surrealistic part of the encounter began. Nowak related that he could see an *opening* in the object through which orange spheres were floating out. Approaching the witnesses these orange spheres began to transform into cloaked beings. Nowak and the rest of the group noticed two rows of apparently material beings though visible only from their waists up, with each one having a small light ball in front of it. Panicked Nowak, thinking the *War of the Worlds* had just started, turned his radio on and discovered that the same celestial *music* played on all frequencies! Then he grasped a sheet of paper and just in case wrote: *"We have been abducted by a UFO."* Who knows what would have happened to them if it were not for a motorcyclist who entered the area and whose appearance forced the aliens to retreat.

It may sound funny but the observers were left very agitated after the cigar-shaped UFO's disappearance. They returned Opole and tried to contact the local press. On the next day Nowak, his father and a small number of journalists reappeared on St. Ann's Hill expecting the strange events would manifest themselves once again. Cameras waited in vain. Nothing happened though Nowak claimed to see some objects (but the rest did not). At one point it is alleged that he was in such a deep shock that he supposedly could not even recognise his own father! But that was just the initial stage of his apparent 'UFO madness'. Too scared to sleep alone, he stayed at his parents. Peering through a balcony window Nowak could see the eyes and contours of a cloaked alien being that was hovering outside remaining visible only to him. Then he fainted. In a state of shock, he retold his entire story to journalists on very the next day. On the night of 20th July, Nowak was still staying at his parents and enjoyed the company of a friend who also had witnessed the strange objects several nights before. They soon experienced another rash of terrifying events and reported seeing dark shadows visible against the walls. Mr. Grzegorz claimed that he could recognise the beings met upon St. Ann's Hill. His mental condition badly deteriorated and on that night he was unable to sleep. But on the next day, a week after the initial visit at the hill, it all ceased and his disturbed psychological state of mind returned to normal.

It may be said that the whole incident was just a mystification or the result of mass hysteria of fantasy-prone minds (with Nowak's role as the leader). The story evoked some real doubts, strengthened by fact that St. Ann's hill is not a deserted area. Was the incident witnessed by any other independent onlookers? The answer is *probably*. It turned out that local Fire Brigade had been notified of some strange lights over the local fields and who had acknowledged the observation of some anomalies. Zagórski, who was engaged in the research of this case, said that any conclusion was *'pending'* and it needed yet further research. But it is now surely too late. Unanswered questions and too many coincidences made the case suspicious to some researchers. Regardless of Nowak's temporary state of *shock* and other unclear psychological elements, it is hard to comprehend why the witnesses did not try to get some photographs (while Nowak claims to experienced further encounters). Moreover, the celestial music heard on the car radio resembles a cheap science-fiction scenario (it sounds in total like a simplified variation of the movie *Close Encounters*). But the most debated aspect of this case is that Nowak was the man who gave the most detailed description of the event despite their being many other witnesses.

Nonetheless, it must be remembered that the reports of Nowak's acquaintances also included many anomalous details. So, in issuing the last sentence on this case may be a challenging task. Maybe it all was just an involuntary, psychologically-driven hysteria. Or maybe it was something too exotic to comprehend?

Nadarzyce incident

Gazeta Poznańska (*Poznań Newspaper*) issue on the 10th of October 1994 was probably the first source reporting that residents living in Nadarzyce and soldiers from the local military range observed "an unidentified object about 300 feet in diameter, had been hovering 1000 feet overhead. Lights on its perimeter suggested that it was a sphere or ellipse. One light beam was directed down towards the town" Soon rumors spread that the military not only tried to intercept the gigantic UFO but even made a *top secret* video documenting the encounter. Surprisingly, the latter assumption turned out to be true but what in fact all of them witnessed on that autumn night is still unknown.

It all started at 8 pm, on October 8th 1994 when residents of Nadarzyce village adjacent to the 21st Central Air Force Range (biggest one in Europe), noticed unidentified lights in the sky. The overall total number of witnesses was hard to estimate but it involved several dozens of military personnel. Reports varied considerably but locals explained that the object was constantly changing shape.

"It took many forms" – Wanda P. from Nadarzyce said.

"At one moment it resembled a square with luminous balls along its perimeter, but then it became a triangle or ellipse. On the inside of all of this was an enormous ball consisting of numerous bright points of light."

From a soldiers' point of view, the Nadarzyce spherical UFO was surrounded by a dozen smaller objects forming a ring around it. Attempts to take photographs of the object resulted in images of a very bad quality although a video made by one of the spectators was allegedly sent to the Air Force Command in Poznań.

Official information from military sources concerning this encounter was a complete mess and only led to a mixture of controversial claims. According to information in the *Polska Zbrojna* (*Armed Poland*) newspaper, the first reports of the sighting came from an officer on duty at the Nadarzyce range. In reaction to this initial report, Krzesiny AFB sent two MiG-21s to intercept the UFO. Rumor's claimed that during their ascent, both of the MiG's experienced a serious of technical malfunctions. According to another version, the object then shot off and disappeared. The most interesting aspect of the Nadarzyce encounter was that the Polish Army for the first (and probably last) time after 1989, engaged officially in an alleged UFO incident. There was an interrogation of both military and civilian witnesses to the event but sadly no direct conclusions emerged. *Polska Zbrojna* quoted Major Eugeniusz Mleczak who stated that the weird phenomenon "was an anomaly of physical origin and pilots are told every year that they may encounter it in autumn".

It is difficult to comment on something like this but soon the case took two new unexpected turns. The first of these were sightings of the same object in Nadarzyce area as well as in other parts of the region. A day before the main sighting, in Biskupice (located dozens of kilometers to south-east); Jerzy Bulczyński and his family at 10 pm saw two identical, gigantic orbs with rotating rings consisting of much smaller spheres, all celadon-gray in color and around 6-8 times bigger than the full moon in size. Sightings of other strange aerial objects, *celestial carousels* or *luminous rings of light* also came from many other locations.

But when the Nadarzyce UFO incident gained notoriety, a quite unexpected explanation emerged. The local TV station broadcast an interview with the director of the Olimpia Circus who claimed that their laser spotlight had caused the UFO rumors. On the night of 7th and 8th October the circus was stationed in Jelenino and the reflector had been in use. At first glance it could explain all the mess but object seemed solid, no light beacons accompanied the sighting and the cloud cover, necessary for that effect was not present according to witnesses from Nadarzyce. Moreover, press reports suggested that the object was maneuvering or even making attempts to land. The Nadarzyce incident would transform into yet another ufological legend but the efforts of Mr. Mariusz Fryckowski who re-analysed the case and quoted the opinion of ufologist Bogdan Grzywna who had viewed the fabled video taken by one of the soldiers. He remarked that it was several minutes long and unclear, maybe due to fact that the author was strongly agitated. But in his opinion, no further speculations were necessary. It was all clear.

"The official Army conclusion was that the sighting was caused by the circus spotlight though further research was needed to confirm this. But that was probably all the Army have ever done and that no further research was conducted despite these recommendations. We can assume that the sighting was caused by Olimpia circus spotlight indeed. Of course others can search for proof that A UFO was the culprit but in my opinion this would all be in vain. My hypothesis can be strengthened by fact that in 1997, in the same region, more spotlights provoked wild gossip once again..."

This case must be marked as closed.

QUOTATIONS SOURCES

Damian Trela Archives / *Czastajemnic.blogspot.com*

Piotr Cielebiaś and Michał Kuśnierz Archives / *infra.org.pl*

Janusz Zagórski Archive / *januszzagorski.pl*

Fryckowski M., *Incydent w Nadarzycach*, infra.org.pl (fragment of non-published book *UFO to tylko pretekst*).

Gołaszewska G., UFO nad Nadarzycami, Gazeta Poznańska, 10/10/1994.

Chapter 13

EXOTIC BOOMERANGS AND FLYING TRIANGLES

Technological mystery or real anomaly? • Giant from Sandomierz and Aarhus
Broken flying triangle over the highway? • Exotic craft over Hrubieszów
Boomerang over Lubliniec estate and astronomer UFO sightings
Baborów "Star Wars" UFO and other oddities

THE USA is literally being haunted by reports of so-called flying triangles and boomerangs which have continued to be reported for several decades now but you may be surprised by the fact that this same phenomenon is manifesting itself in many different parts of Poland as well. The sightings are of matching characteristics and pose identical questions. Although reports of those objects have been circulating for several decades, no plausible explanation has yet emerged.

"Are they a secret military technological mystery *per se* or real anomaly?" – One of cardinal questions to ask. One can find arguments backing up both of these proposals. A number of interesting ideas on these reports has originated with the National Institute of Discovery Science (NIDS) whose evaluation of flying triangles was published in 2004.

"Neither the agenda nor the origin of the Flying Triangles are currently known" – they wrote, although other comments highlighted a possibility that those objects form a class of new, ultra-advanced airships equipped with sophisticated, soundless propulsion systems.

But some patterns in flying triangles/boomerangs sightings are consistent with the overall features of the wider UFO phenomenon. These objects appear in a great variety, often over highly populated areas and demonstrate advanced technological capabilities with no desire to make direct contact. In other words, the main task of these objects is to show up, shock the witnesses and disappear, just as flying saucers seem to do. This makes no sense if this technology involves secret military hardware that is man made by whichever nation on Earth. The growing popularity of unmanned drones casts some new light on the flying triangles/boomerang mystery but it is rather hard to allocate them to that group. The RQ-170 Sentinel is one of the biggest drones that could be blamed for the reports of weird boomerang-shaped UFOs over Poland but the witnesses reported these objects to be of nearly gigantic dimensions, usually operating at a very low altitude and very close to ground level. But the most exotic part of the boomerang sightings was that all the reports mentioned non-typical, in fact a quite absurd form of camouflage.

"Clearly visible camouflage" and broken triangle over the highway

We have mentioned a few early examples of triangular UFO sightings from the 1960s and the 1980s but they were occasional and little is known about them. The contemporary wave of complex and reliable reports started in 2008 with the Sandomierz sighting. It must be stressed that the mutual classification of flying triangles and boomerang UFOs is rather arbitrary. I have based it on the conclusion that both groups with their potential resemblance to products of human technology, can stem from the same source. But in fact there is third class of these objects of a more complicated shape loosely based on a flying wing design or of a triangular construction.

Probably the first report of a camouflaged *misty boomerang-shaped object* after 1999 (year of Poland's accession to NATO) occurred on November 16th 2002 in the Old Town district of Rzeszów. This little known sighting was followed by several years with no known sightings at all going on the record. This lack of reports of the flying triangle came to an end in early November 2008 when Mr. Piotr G. – an architect from Sandomierz (świętokrzyskie) contacted us saying that he observed a very strange craft resembling a boomerang or half-moon with bright contours and red dots on its inside. It was about 6 pm on October 31st when the witness left his parents house and decided to call his wife. At that moment he accidentally looked at the sky noticing something moving. Then he saw a *technological wonder* in motion.

> *"The edges of the object were a little fuzzy or camouflaged. For me they looked as if made of dirty, muddy waving water. The object's body looked as if it was surrounded with some sort of a white-red field of mist. It seemed to me that the mist was dotted with numerous red points of light. The object came from the south-west and was heading north-east at tremendous great speed and simultaneously in complete silence"* – Mr. Piotr said.

"Its size was very impressive. The object's wingspan was approximately equal to the full Moon in diameter and despite it being surrounded by the mist it could be clearly seen outlined against the velar sky. I must say that I was both anxious and excited. I realised that the object represents some kind of technology that is far in advance of anything on Earth and it was clear to me that it was built by some form of intelligence. I have not seen anything like this in all my life and it was not a plane, satellite or meteor."

In 2011 I was contacted by Mrs. Krystyna C. – A Polish citizen living in Aarhus (Denmark) who read about Mr. Piotr's sighting and she wanted to share a nearly identical report of a silent boomerang-shaped object that she had personally witnessed in early November 2008. She saw it at about 9 or 10 pm when she went outside to smoke a cigarette.

"The weather conditions were typical for a November night, with few clouds in the sky. At one point moment I looked up and saw a gigantic object. Its contours were surrounded with a kind of illumination, luminescence or whatever… It was moving very slowly. The object was heading west. It is hard for me to describe the object composition that looked like glass or jelly that was moving and was illuminated but not with any points of light. Nevertheless, when I realised the object's dimensions and structure, I became quite frightened. It struck me that they could be omnipresent and invisible to people even in the daytime. It was just by chance that I looked up and saw this giant object."

There is no doubt that witnesses in different cities separated by nearly 620 miles saw virtually identical objects. Both witnesses mentioned the odd kind of camouflage that made the object visible and both were puzzled by this large objects apparent lack of noise. (The only difference included points of light mentioned in Sandomierz sighting.)

The boomerangs were about to return to Poland in 2013 but late 2008 also brought some more reports of the flying triangles. One of the most interesting cases allegedly involved an academic teacher from Sulejówek (mazowieckie) who stated that on November 17th, during a stroll with dog, he came across an unidentified triangular object with lights positioned along its rounded edges and at its center. In the witness' opinion the object flew directly over him. Unfortunately, he refused further interviews so his sighting is sadly of little research significance but still remains one of interest. One of the most spectacular sightings did however take place on September 16th, at about 10:30 pm, when Michał D. was returning home with his fiancée. Driving along the highway between Częstochowa and Łódź, in the Wikłów area, he noticed large a craft hovering just over the road.

> "We were 12-18 miles north of Częstochowa. I saw a black triangle with lights at its corners slowly floating over the highway. At first I took it for the emergency landing of an airplane. Then I realised it was something different. When it emerged from behind a hill it was clear that the object was in the shape of a perfect triangle. It was moving very slowly. Two of the three lights were shining with constant light but one was blinking, as if defective. When I passed below the object (it came over the road so it was inevitable), I managed to catch a glimpse of its propulsion system (?) or the hull of the object. It turned out not to be smooth at all but with side parts covered with some protuberances (cubical and similar). Anyway, its bottom part seemed smooth" – Michał D. reported. According to the witness's estimates, the object was nearly the same size of the width of the road, i.e. 30 feet and it was a deep black color. The observer could not calculate its exact flight level but it was around 500 feet in the air. "It looked like a gas ring" – he described the alleged propulsion system. "In each corner the object possessed a circle comprising of small spouts. Flames or light emanated from them which shone out sideways."

Mr. Michał mentioned that in the first phase of the sighting the object seemed to be in a slow rotating motion. It took two passes over the highway and despite the late night hour the highway had a fair amount of traffic on it and there is no doubt that other drivers saw it too. In Mr. Michał's opinion, he could see other cars decelerating when the triangle passed over the road. According to him, when the object flew over the hills adjacent to the highway, it made a turn and took another pass over the road but at much higher altitude. On that occasion all the *nozzles* shone with a constant light.

Nearly half a year later in Poznań, a witness from the Łazarz district took a very indistinct photographic image of an alleged flying triangle hovering in the south-western sector of the sky. "At first I took it for an illusion. It was twilight and the sky was not so dark. The weather was good with high clouds and in the background I noticed the triangle. I managed to snap two photos. It is also interesting to note that when the object departed, pair of F-16 appeared from Krzesiny AFB."

Let us pause for a moment. In the NIDS evaluation of the flying triangles phenomenon it was mentioned that they had a tendency to appear in vicinity of military installations. Poznań holds the Krzesiny Air Force Base, Sandomierz holds The Radio Technical Brigade (already mentioned in previous chapters) while at Sulejówek is the Military Automobile Institute. Other sightings also took place in locations connected with military installations. The same applies to Hrubieszów (lubelskie) in south-eastern Poland that holds the 2nd Reconnaissance Brigade. The witness to that sighting requested full anonymity and restricted any contact only to an exchange via e-mail. He claimed that his position in local community prevented him from revealing his personal details but his report was full and detailed, proving that he was well oriented in the local topography and military technologies which may indicate that he has (or had) a military background. The sighting took place on August 20th, at about 4:45 pm., a mile from the cities suburbs.

> *"At 10-15 degrees over the western horizon I saw a triangular object which looked as if it was made of a silvery metal. It was rotating around its axis but remained stationary. The entire sighting was 12 minutes long. Based on visual estimates and the comparison between the object and the local buildings I came to the conclusion that the minimum length of its side was more than 50 feet. It was located 1.2-1.8 miles away and seemed to be very large in size. I completely excluded the possibility that the object could be some European or American military drone. Its behavior in the air was not consistent with any conventional aircraft. It was devoid of rotors or jet engines and seemed to be a uniform metal object without any elements indicating the presence of propulsion systems known in military or civilian aviation circles. Because I am also interested in astronomy and astrophysics, I can exclude the possibilities that the sighting was caused by any celestial objects as well or the ISS (International Space Station). Therefore no natural or man-made objects can be responsible for the observation. Added to this, the object flew over at a very low altitude around just 330 feet."*

The witness also mentioned that around this time a number of military exercises took place over Hrubieszów where a radiolocation unit is based. This object resembled an isosceles triangle with some convexities in upper and lower part and disappeared in a very unusual manner. The witness related that at one point the object dimmed and literally vanished in mid-air in matter of seconds. The Army denied any knowledge of the sighting and stated that the object was nothing to do with them.

The Triangular Flap of 2013 and the Ukrainian trail

After many months of calmness, boomerangs and triangles returned in the summer of 2013. From today's perspective it is apparent that their emergence preceded the Ukrainian crisis, unrest on the eastern NATO border and the strengthening of USAF garrisons in Poland. But then the Polish ufological community was shaken by a number of reports of large aerial vessels seen over smaller cities and villages, with three (but unrelated) sightings culminating on the night of August 3rd.

The summer flap had been preceded by a strange incident in Biała village (dolnośląskie) at the turn of May and April in 2013. Damian Trela who collected the accounts of a young couple, Magda and Tomasz, claims that at twilight they observed a set of triangular over a local forest.

> *"At first I saw a flat formation of three lights. They emerged from behind the forest and stopped in the air. After a while the object was stationary and at that moment I realised that it was shaped like an isosceles triangle. I immediately called my wife"* – Krzysztof said.

Her description of the object varied considerably but it might be caused by Mrs. Magda's eyesight which was said to be pretty poor. Nevertheless she managed to snap a photo with her cell-phone camera that unfortunately was too weak to produce anything of any quality. But Damian's estimations based on the eyewitnesses' accounts suggest that the object could have been more than 400 feet in diameter. After a change of position in the sky it moved off in the direction of Chojnów.

On the evening of August 3rd from 10:30 to 11pm, witnesses reported three successive sightings of unidentified, triangular objects but with differing descriptions. The first report came from M. (name withheld) – a woman from Lubliniec (śląskie) who is the wife of a soldier with the local Special Forces unit. She reported that at about 10:30 pm, she went for a stroll with her dog. While walking her dog she noticed a gigantic boomerang-shaped craft floating over her housing estate. As in previous cases, the boomerang seemed partially camouflaged.

> *"At first I took it for some starry mirage but it was floating overhead very slowly and low over the ground"* – she informed us.

> *"I was amazed with the complete lack of any sound. The lights of the craft were dim and were the same color as the stars and were placed symmetrically along the object. The objects contour at first glance could not be distinguished from the background of the sky. At first I thought that it was transparent but I focused on a star which soon it became obscured as the object blocked it from view. The object looked like a computer-generated image. Only the lights on its surface seemed clearly visible. I would add that it was flying westwards, directly over the house on 1000-lecia 2 Street."*

The woman found it difficult to assess the objects flight level (in fact it is hard even for experienced people, especially at night) but she said that it was at *"four heights of the apartment house"* what is equal to less than 150 feet above the ground! Because it was passing directly over the estate, she could compare the UFO's length to that of a building. In her opinion it must have been about 65 feet in length. The object was barely visible to the human eye thanks to its masking that was also interestingly described by Mrs. M. In her own words, it was *"similar to that used in movies when they want to show that something is both visible and invisible"* (she probably referred to that type of camouflage that could be seen in *Predator or Star Trek*).

If the woman's report and all of her valuations were accurate then it was another instance of boomerangs/triangles recklessness and violation of all possible safety rules as it was flying at such a low altitude.

The next example took place during a similar sighting on October 13th 2013 that was witnessed by Mr. Mateusz from Pabianice (łódzkie).

"Five minutes past midnight, on October 13th, I went to the balcony to smoke a cigarette and noticed a very large object in the night skies. It looked like a group of stars – yellow lights flying at speed over Pabianice, from the northeast to west or from the Łódź area to Łask. It looked like a group of stars covered by some hazy mist or watery glow that formed the boomerang's very large dimensions. We have here a flight corridor for Lublinek airport and Łask AFB. We often see some unusual things in the skies but this thing was the eeriest of them all. The sighting lasted just a matter of seconds. When it had disappeared, I tried to woke up my wife. The unidentified object was curved as a sort of boomerang or paraglider. It was semi-transparent. Lights and contours were not clear but the glow emanated from the object made it clearly visible" – he said.

Reports of this kind forced ufologist to ask a question: "Who is undertaking such risky and dangerous low-level flights?" It concerns not only the potential danger of unveiling some covert military operations but also the threat these low flying objects pose to civilians. What would happen, if such an object crashed somewhere between the housing estate in Lubliniec? But let us return to the night of August 3rd when a triangular object was observed by a young couple in Łosice (mazowieckie) near the Polish-Belarusian border. The witness, Mr. M.K. from Warsaw and his girlfriend reported a nighttime sighting of a dark, triangular UFO object with gray-violet colored lights.

Triangular UFO observers included several people trained in astronomy. One of them was an engineer – the last witness from August 3rd. At about 11pm he observed a delta-shaped light formation flying majestically over Dobrzykowice (dolnośląskie) – hundreds of miles away from Łosice.

"I'm a rationalist" – he stressed in an interview with Damian Trela. *"But that sight astounded me. I observed a formation of lights set in a delta-shape, high in the sky. Nine points formed a uniform array, with one light at the front and four on both sides."*

But much more extraordinary account came to me from Mr. Karol M. – an amateur astronomer from the Lublin area who on the night of August 14th was tracking a strange aerial (or rather orbital) object with his telescope. In his detailed account he mentioned that a bright point under close-up revealed a mysterious crimson-red triangle.

"That object's trajectory grabbed my attention. It resembled a rocket or space shuttle's ascending phase. In the night sky only its triangular contour and red color were discernable, with its center looking yellowish. But the object was in the shape of an isosceles triangle. Its color and oscillations resembled flames at first. But the entire triangle was crimson-red in color with another, smaller isosceles triangle inserted symmetrically into it. During the sighting they did not change their positions so it must be a singular object or two items joined together" – Mr. Karol reported. He added that the object was apparently flying into the upper layers of atmosphere. His sighting is still awaiting an explanation.

Other incidents from 2013 flap included amongst others:

- Sokółka (podlaskie), September 9th: A seconds-long flyby of a gigantic triangular UFO witnessed by two adult males from a balcony.
- Warsaw, Hynek Street (mazowieckie), September 12th: Nocturnal sighting of object an identical to that of Dobrzykowice.
- Częstochowa, Osson's Hill (śląskie), August 1st: Nocturnal sighting of an alleged triangular UFO by a group of young people. No exact information available.
- Szklarska Poreba (dolnośląskie), June 19th: Jan W.'s sighting of an alleged triangular UFO with lights in each corner (seen from a distance; possibility of a plane misidentification).

It was hard for ufologists to connect any official military activity (such as exercises) with this flap of triangular or boomerang shaped UFOs sightings. Reports could not have been the result of mass hysteria as the unconnected reports were not covered by the mainstream media. But it was clear that if the objects were of military origin then they would not belong to the poorly funded Polish Air Force. There are several reasons to categorise these objects as advanced American/NATO military airships. Firstly, NIDS conclusions on the flying triangles phenomenon in the United States coincide with our findings on the behavior and characteristics of these objects. Secondly, Poland and the USA cooperate in military-related projects not only under NATO auspices. A long term scandal of alleged illegal CIA prisons on Polish territory is still a hot topic for debate in Poland.

Poland's border with Russia, Ukraine and Belarus also forms NATO easternmost boundary. Is it just a mere coincidence that the flap of a silent and camouflaged object predated the great political revolution of Ukraine that surely was not a spontaneous action but well planned event backed by Western governments? Just a thought. What is the situation now with these flying triangles? And what is their real task? Unfortunately, the great difference in the eyewitnesses' descriptions of these objects is not making the matter any clearer and makes a definitive conclusion almost impossible.

Highly untypical objects

Reports of flying triangles and boomerangs, highly diversified and partially anomalous, represent only two faces of a much more complicated phenomenon. As I have said previously, these objects resemble machines made by human hands and come in great variety. If these were military aircraft, it must mean either every craft is designed and built independently or there is something wrong with the witnesses' observational abilities. The same inexplicable anomaly is haunting the UFO phenomenon in which it is very difficult to compare two stories that depict identical UFOs. The size and shape of allegedly *man-made UFOs* is not confined to triangular or boomerang shaped objects. The catalogue of very untypical military aircraft is very long. If the flying triangles and boomerangs makers' identity remains unknown, then who would be able to build and manipulate these and yet more exotic flying machines?

In rainy August in 2002, 36-year-old Piotr G. stayed with his family in Szczuczyn (podlaskie). He could remember during the next to last day of his vacation, along with two of his friends he went outside to smoke a cigarette. The cloud cover was heavy but spread out along the sky and in one of the clouds openings, just above their heads; the witnesses detected a very unusual, V-shaped machine.

> *"There were strong, brilliant, white lights located at the corners of the craft. The object's angular shape was very clear. All the lights were set symmetrically and the interior of the craft seemed dark. I realised that it would soon go behind the cloud cover in matter of seconds, so I tried to observe as many details as possible. It was moving very slowly, from west to east, with the opened part ahead as if to counter our aerodynamics understanding which assume that the sharpest part must be in front. Unfortunately, it disappeared after short while and left me astounded"* – the witness admitted.

Chris Miekina – A Polish citizen from Sandomierz who now lives in New Jersey – a long-time UFO enthusiast who runs the Nowa Atlantyda (New Atlantis) web portal, received an even more interesting report from 1995. The witness reported that a triangular object "as big as a lorry" appeared over his car he traveling in along with a group of friends. This all took place in the Poznań area.

"It was flying soundlessly and without any stir of the air. What is interesting is that our car radio died out and it restarted by itself when we were about 2 miles from our destination" – he said, adding that the object resembled that object from a famous viral-video with a pyramid-shaped UFO over Moscow.

There were many more strange reports of M-shaped objects. One of several reports came from Kowale Oleckie (warmińsko-mazurskie) near the Russian Kaliningrad Oblast border. The case was reported to WMGU – one of the few local and still active ufological groups with Bogdan Zabielski, late Mieczysław Szczepanik (former Special Services agent) and Arek Kocik.

"On August 21st 2009, at 9:40pm, Mr. Tomasz Skorupski noticed a flying object in the shape of letter M just about 200 feet above ground level. It was floating in the air from west to east. The witness assessed that it was around 110-130 yards away and was entirely deep-black in color, measuring from 10 feet in length to 30 feet at the widest part. Despite its dimensions the object seemed flat as a sheet of paper (according to the witness). There were 7 dimly-yellowish lights positioned on the craft (3 on both arms) while the rest seemed dark and obscured the stars on its flight path. The object was completely silent, moving at a speed of about 50mph" – they wrote.

But probably the most outlandish thing had been observed by an 18-year-old girl from Baborów (opolskie) who on September 25th 2011 called us in a state of great shock saying that about 5am she was awoken by light emanating from a strangely structured craft hovering just outside her bedroom window. She then jumped out of here bed and awoke her brother and father but before they reached the window the strange UFO had managed to move away and was now over nearby fields where it was still visible but in a *changed form*.

"I woke up at about 5am, seeing a kind of brightness that filled my room. At first I took it for moonlight but it was of a blue tint" – she wrote.

"My bed is just by the window. When I looked at that strange craft, initially I thought it was a plane but it was still and too large. It resembled some kind of futuristic vessel from the sci-fi movies (I'm not interested in this genre). The craft's contours were outlined with white pointed lights and there was something like a hatch in its central part. From that opening for a short while a white light or mist was emanating. The entire object was bluish in color. I was frightened and felt I was in danger. I quickly jumped out of my bed and went to get my brother" – she reported.

The object departed west but did not disappear until about 6:30am. When their father joined them the UFO was just a bright point in the sky, ejecting down some brilliant yellowish lights. I observed the object with my binoculars, it looked like it was composed of some *"dense, sticky light"* – one of the family said. All the witnesses corroborated the event and stated that they even tried to take photo of the strange manifestation but it was obviously too far away for a good quality snap with their cell-phone camera.

Witnesses of the Baborów sighting were simple people from a small town, afraid of media attention and their neighbors' opinions (after publication of a report at our website, they demanded it to be withdrew but then we reach a compromise). Certainly the most interesting part of the encounter was the female witness' sighting of a structured, *bus-sized* craft. It is worth mentioning that in her opinion the bluish light radiated heat similar to that of sunbeams. She could feel it on her face and forehead as if the luminosity wad aimed to wake her up – she stated.

"The craft was generally of a triangular shape, with slightly wider, wing-like structures in the middle and back. In the center of the bottom part there was a kind of hatch. There were also whitish halogen-like lights around its perimeter. A pair of red-orange lights was positioned behind the hatch" – the woman reported. *"Trying to awake my brother, I was permanently looking at that direction. But when he reached the window, in just seconds, the craft turned back and disappeared, changing into a big white light somewhere in the distance."*

From our point of view the Baborów craft resembled the cross-section of a chess pawn with an angular hatch in the flat bottom part. Although we received reports from that area concerning some *strange aerial lights*, no one mentioned a structured, bluish craft. So was it just a dream from delusional of 18-year-old girl? She refused this possibility saying she could also see the object when she was fully awake. Without question the incident she took part in was one of the most mysterious UFO encounters in recent years. Most recent UFO sighting of man-made looking UFOs involved a group sighting of a structured craft resembling a rose cup, which took place on August 18th 2013. Members of family owning a dacha in Tyczyn (podkarpackie), at about 7 pm noticed the maneuvers of small silvery object. Observing it with binoculars, they noticed it resembled a wingless *aerial probe* consisting of spear-shaped panels set on a dish-like base.

"The sky was clear and cloudless and the object moved very slowly, without making a sound. I showed it to my brother. My second brother and his wife also became interested in it and I asked them for their binoculars and camera.

At some point the object was blinking with a light, as if it was in a rotating motion and reflecting sunlight" – he said.

For ground-based observers it was very hard to notice the object since it was making constant turns and ascents. At some point, the main witness lost it from view but then it reappeared. He also managed to take a photo of the object but unfortunately it looks just a bright dot in the sky.

Cases like these presented above only deepen the flying triangles/boomerangs mystery. Although all the mentioned objects resemble products of human technology, their behavior and capabilities exhibit many as yet unknown technologies. Providing that these objects activity constitute a part of a wide ranging military test or some other covert activities, their apparent careless tactics including exposing themselves to the eyewitnesses is very hard to explain. So it is possible to compare them to the general flying saucers phenomenon? Or maybe some party is doing their best to persuade us that these objects are not what they seem to be?

QUOTATIONS SOURCES

Damian Trela Archives / *Czastajemnic.blogspot.com*

Arek Miazga Archives / Arekmiazga.blogspot.com.

Piotr Cielebiaś and Michał Kuśnierz Archives / *infra.org.pl*

Chapter 14

FLYING SAUCER INCIDENTS OF 2010

**Flying disc and military helicopters • Mothers shocked by a UFO
No straight answer from AFB • Family goes beneath a flying saucer**

IT is a lie that flying saucers are all in the proverbial ufological past. A series of events from March 2010 has convinced us that even in an era of digital photography, information technology and cell-phone cameras; there are phenomena and events' appearing that is out of the range of human awareness and a plethora of electronic surveillance. In other words, many people today are convinced that the entire population is under constant electronic supervision and that the authorities can see everything we do. However those alleged UFO incidents that involve people who apparently disappear without a trace or aircraft that disappear would cause the powers-that-be to perhaps change their mind.

Now in one of the last chapters of my book I have devoted this chapter to looks at what we might term as classic cases of the UFO phenomenon. I decided that the final chapters would be dedicated to high-strangeness and the more unusual UFO cases that in recent years became areas of increased interest to both me and other researchers here in Poland. The events described below also could not be labeled as *'normal'* UFO *sightings but they do instead display a number of common elements reported in other such incidents.*

A short but spectacular chain of events took place from March 2011 but unfortunately it did not provide any good photographic evidence to accompany it. Overall, there is a growing problem with present-day UFO photos and videos. Despite widespread use of cell-phones with cameras, most photos of unidentified objects leave much to be desired. Of course in the early years of the digital photography era, most ufologists (including me) were perplexed with mysterious disc-like forms on photos that remained invisible to the photographers. Today we do not accept reports containing these so called '*chance UFOs*' or *Blurfos* any more but on the other hand we do face serious questions concerning the lack of authentic photographic evidence in the wake of intensified UFO activity.

I think it is important to stress that more and more of the contemporary UFO witnesses do try to take photographs during their sightings and encounters. Unfortunately, most of them are neither professional photographers nor owners of any high quality equipment capable of capturing clear images of distant objects (with majority of sightings taking place at night). In the case of the 2010 saucer wave, two groups of witnesses had unique opportunities to photograph UFOs at a very close range. But sadly they failed. All of those involved admitted that when they found themselves directly below these apparent exotic objects, they thought about their children's safety in the first place and not about taking a photograph.

Saucer invading the airport area in Kraków

A series of UFO sightings including successive nighttime incidents in the Kraków and Rzeszów area, took place from the 8th to 12th of March 2010. Dozen's of independent witnesses reported their observations to me and Arek Miazga all describing encounters with a classical flying saucer illuminated with colorful lights. In two instances groups of witnesses drove their cars beneath the object which provided them with an ideal close-up view of the object. This series of events began on March 8th, at about 7:20pm in Łyczanka (a village south of Kraków) when a flying disc with white lights along perimeter flew over the road:

> "*It was flying very slowly and had green and red lights underneath. It was flying 100-160 feet over the road and made a slow rotating movement. I could not believe my eyes and stopped the car. I turned the radio off but could not hear any noise from the flying machine! I saw it clearly and so did my daughter. The object was about 50 feet across. A number of military helicopters appeared over the area*" – a 38-year-old man reported.

In his opinion the UFO disappeared heading west. Two hours after that sighting, nearly 15 miles to the north-east from Łyczanka, two women and their children experienced a terrifying event when they confronted a saucer-like craft hovering over the road close to Balice Airport. The adult witnesses (respectively 38- and 39-year-old) requested full anonymity due to their professional status.

> "*After driving down the Kraków-Katowice highway we drove along a straight stretch of road with Balice Airport to our right. We soon noticed some strong, bright lights over the road (the sky was clear that night) and we were sure that it was nothing more than an aircraft coming into land. But when we approached*

the object and it was directly above us, we looked up and saw a symmetrical, metallic saucer with red lights along perimeter! We passed beneath it and then for a short period I continued to observe it from the car's left hand side window. I don't know whether it was the same object that changed position or another machine. We were in such a state of shock that we did not stop to snap a photo. I do not know if it was some sort of military object or apparatus but it was round and evidently metallic" – said the woman from passenger seat.

Her friend (who drove the car) added another perplexing detail. In her opinion the object was at first a strong light but then somehow it changed into a metallic looking flying saucer. In the passenger's opinion, the UFO was about 20-25 feet across with a uniform coating devoid of any features typical of conventional aircraft. For the driver, its hull seemed composed of some sort of heavy metal. During the sighting the object stayed at an altitude of less than 150 feet. Both women estimate that the duration of the sighting was quite short and that the UFO may have turned and moved away as when they looked back it was nowhere to be seen.

Sightings continued on the next day in the same area. Another woman who was also driving her car with children on the backseat claimed that a circular object with ring of white lights (resembling *light bulbs*) passed over her car at 6:30pm in Kryspinów, some 2 miles south from location of the previous encounter. The UFO stopped for a moment and then departed to the north, toward Balice Airport. Just 10 minutes later a woman from the Bronowice Nowe district of Kraków (2 miles east from the airport), during a stroll with her dog also witnessed the flight of a disc-shaped object surrounded with ring of white light:

"I saw a light ring with a diameter comparable to that of an aircraft. It was quite thin. The object was low over the ground and its lights seemed unstable (but not twinkling). Inside of the circle I saw a dark space and realised that the object must be inclined and I could see its bottom part with two large, steady lights, one green and one red " – she stated adding that a vibrating sound could also be heard.

In summary: numerous witnesses reported seeing a strange disc-shaped object of considerable size with white or red lights on its perimeter and red-green lights on the bottom part. There was only one instance where the eyewitness mentioned any sounds generated by the objects.

UFO activity touched the outlying areas of Cracow very close to the local airport. Officially named John Paul II International Airport Kraków-Balice it lies adjacent to the 8th Air Force Base (now 8th Base of Air Transport). Some may take this as hint as to the possible origin of these reports. I received two official responses from the base commander's office informing me that "no *special missions* took place from the military airfield on 8th and 9th of March. The regular function of the base was not interrupted in any way" and "no *extraordinary* events took place on the dates in question". In other words the Air Force was not responsible for the sightings.

I fully expected this response from them but it is surprising that the Polish Air Force did not react to the abnormal aerial activity in their airspace. Kraków – the capital city of the Polish Kingdom is the second biggest Polish city and a popular tourist destination. Who would risk cruising at such a low altitude in any kind of exotic man-made aircraft breaking all safety rules and disclosing its presence to the general population? The same questions apply of course to the unidentified triangles/boomerangs sightings. A director of the civilian air authorities at Balice also issued a statement explaining that their area of interest is restricted to airspace over the airport and that on 8th-9th of March they did not register any unauthorised violations or incidents that might corroborate the eyewitnesses' reports.

The official impasse that arose is the typical response from the authorities in Poland when responding to enquiries on UFO sightings with no one officially taking the responsibility to answer any specific questions concerning the nature and origin of these sightings. The people who came across the object knew that waiting for an official response would be fruitless so they forwarded their reports and questions to me and my colleagues. We do of course appreciate this but they also have the right to be officially informed by both the state and military services that we all sustain when paying our taxes.

Rzeszów sightings

Three days after the Kraków sightings, a flying saucer invaded the area of the Brzezówka village – just west of Arek Miazga's hometown. Amongst numerous reports, there was one incident that stood out that involved a family who during a return from church on March 12th encountered a dull-gray, saucer-like UFO hovering over road from Dębica to Ropczyce.

> *"At about 7 pm, in the area of hill in Brzezówka, along with my wife and kids I noticed something that at first I took for a plane coming into land. 'Look! It descended so low on its way to Jasionka airfield' – I said to them but after about 10 seconds I realised that our car was quickly approaching the object. Passing beneath it, we recognised that it was not an airplane at all. It had red lights on the bottom part, surrounding a big cupola which was emitting a green light. The object's color resembled dull nichrome while its hull looked like it was split into different segments. Realising this, I decided to turn back and to take some photographs but the object began to drift away in the direction*

of Okonin. It then accelerated and we lost it from sight. If it was some sort of conventional aircraft, at such altitude, surely a tremendous roar and gush of air or fumes would have hit us…" – the 35-year-old witness related to Arek.

He also added during the interview that the segments were visible only on the left hand side of the saucer. The UFO's covering looked as if comprised of uneven puzzles with a band of rectangular lights on the bottom part encircling a green protuberance or cupola.

According to estimations, the saucer was hovering less than 150 feet overhead and its dimensions were really jaw dropping. It was much wider than the road and according to Arek Miazga's calculations; it may have been around 45 feet in diameter! After driving for a quarter of mile, the witness' wife encouraged him to return and take a photograph of the object. During this second approach the stationary object now began to accelerate and departed in direction of the Okonin forests. Convinced that there must be other witnesses to the sighting, Arek made a request for information in the local press. He received several interesting responses including a possible corroboration of the incident by a group of independent witnesses who shortly before 7pm on March 12th drove the same way and who also observed a circular, dark object with colorful lights hovering over the road in Lubzina – the next village west from Brzezówka.

But what is interesting is that a number of witnesses also mentioned that there was military helicopter activity in the area. From the flight control of the local Jasionka airport, the researcher found out that at the time of the UFO sighting an MI-8 military helicopter was in the air but they denied any knowledge of any mysterious craft. Arek decided to ask for more details and he received the following response: "Unfortunately, we cannot disclose details on aerial operations of the Polish Armed Forces."

So what did the military *operation* involve? Arek Miazga is sure that the people he interviewed could not simply be delusional. But a decades old unwritten law of the Polish Air Force prevents any laymen from obtaining any information on any of its internal affairs. There are even laws today in Poland that does not permit anyone to write about any activities of the Polish military and attempts to prosecute these that do have been mixed.

It is perhaps worthy here to mention certain details connected with the saucer incidents in general. At first it should be noted that despite many similarities between the objects from Kraków and Brzezówka, descriptions of their bottom sections as well as the hull covering varied considerably. It is also worth considering that in contrary to older reports, contemporary close encounters with both saucers and flying triangles etc, do not provoke any apparent side-effects on electronic equipment, car engines and human behavior. They UFOs also show no tendencies for sudden disappearances and other paranormal effects. Does this mean that UFO phenomenon has changed intentionally? Or perhaps those who design man-made aircraft have simply mimicked the outward appearance of UFOs for their own secret reasons?

QUOTATION SOURCES

Arek Miazga Archives / Arekmiazga.blogspot.com.

Piotr Cielebiaś and Michał Kuśnierz Archives / *infra.org.pl*

Chapter 15

POLICE OFFICERS GO ON THE RECORD

Senior corporal contra cigar-shaped UFO • Oblong object over the glass factory • Close encounter with intelligently-controlled spheres Saucer vs. patrol car • Officers' missing time episode?

THE Polish Police Force also has its unwritten internal code of conduct .In recent years they have publicised their many successes but have also kept silent over some of its failings. Most individual police officers prefer not to criticise its failing but simply toe the party line. What we would like to know is do Polish police officers, like their American counterparts, deal with UFO sightings reported to them? The unofficial answer is *yes* though officially UFOS do not exist. For many decades officers have remained silent but several of them could not keep quiet forever and decided to reveal their own experiences, sometimes frightening, sometimes perplexing. But according to a number of officers the overall number of police officers experiencing UFO encounters while on duty is quite high.

Little is known about such encounters prior to 1989 as it was the time of the State Police (called Civilian Militia) – which was much more efficient than today's equivalent. Sadly there are only a few known details concerning such UFO sightings with Mr. Jerzy K.'s (a police officer) close encounter being the most complex one. It took place in February 1978, three months before Jan Wolski's case, during a night patrol between Ornontowice and Chudów in the Silesian region.

"It happened at about 2 am. I was a senior corporal of the State Police. On that night I was ordered to patrol the Ornontowice-Chudów area. To be exact, my duties were restricted to checking if the local shops were properly secured" – he informed us. *"I was on foot patrol and not in a vehicle. I could remember that*

the night was excellent for walking. It was only minus 5 degrees with a sky clear. I was half-way to my destination when I noticed that my dog, Jazgot, was acting strangely. Because I could not see anything that might upset him, I instinctively looked up hearing at the same time some unusual sounds. I then noticed a large 'thing' passing through the air at a quite low level. It was a kind of cigar, all black and I had the impression that there were small windows along its central section and that someone was observing me through them! It could not be a plane (it was alike to AN-22 hull but without any wings). No loud engine sounds permeated the air but I could hear a slight humming sound similar to Hoover vacuum cleaner. I could see the entire object against the night sky. Then I observed it from behind as it departed in the direction of Bytom. From that angle it looked like a dark circle in the sky. Afraid that I had already witnessed a plane crash, I immediately called the officer on-duty in the Gierałtowice police station, asking about any other reports. He scoffed at me saying that upon my return I must pass a sobriety test!"

Mr. Jerzy then called the local airport but was informed that they had no aircraft airborne at the time. With regards to his feeling of being stared at, he explained that he could not see any passengers in the cigar-shaped object. It was just a weird sensation; maybe it was the same sensation that spooked his dog?

This case of a police officer and a flying cigar is a fitting point to highlight an incident from the summer of 2004 that was witnessed by a former police officer and then a security guard at the Częstochowa Glass Factory, Mr. Jan K. (58) and his colleague Mieczysław Ś. (62). The first of these two men stated that he witnessed on two consecutive nights a large oblong-shaped object with two brightly lit yellow, *egg-like lights* on both ends that flew just 90 feet above their guard post.

The most interesting police officers sightings after 1989 come from the Opole area, with the most recent one involving a pair of witnesses who in January 2013 came across a large disc-shaped craft during night patrol in a small village which is lost amongst the forests of Nysa. Their case highlighted the official reaction of the Polish Police Force to the UFO phenomenon. It was no ordinary sighting but also had many elements of high-strangeness about it as well.

Saucer stalking a police car

Before we proceed to the Nysa incident, let us check another close encounter of a pair of Opole officers that took place in the summer of 1997 in the village of Daniec. Although the main witness changed profession, he prefers to remain anonymous.

"It was in June or July 1997, at night. I was at the time a colour sergeant in the Opole Police. With my partner, Sergeant X, we received an emergency call

Artist interpretation of the UFO incident involving a Police patrol car in the Opole area in January 2013. (Credit: Sebastian Yoszko Woszczyk / Infra.org.pl Archives)

from the duty sergeant with a drunken man terrorising people in a village near Opole. When we reached the location, my partner stopped the police car by a field as he had to use the lavatory. I also got out of the car for a second to stretch my legs. At the same time I noticed that thing and heard my colleague screaming: 'Look up! UFOs!' I saw two bright spheres maneuvering about 330 yards to left of our car. They were extraordinary and unexplainable. The objects were engaged in a chaotic motion – stopped and then accelerated, making sharp turns in the air. We were totally shocked with what we saw! All of a sudden one of the spheres came closer and was just a dozen of yards away! The other one was still circling over the field. In a fraction of a second both departed at high speed. Their behavior left me with no doubt that they were intelligently controlled. "I have never seen anything like this before or since."

The incident witnessed on January 8th 2013 (Tuesday) by a pair of policemen from the Opole area became much more controversial. Their strange encounter with a flying machine in the classic form of a flying saucer resulted in more questions than answers. Although I know the witnesses personal data and affiliation, I have decided not to reveal this information, being aware that it may affect their careers and private life. Moreover, in contrary to other Police UFO observers, our informants immediately reported their experience to their principals. The main witness to these events is a young officer called Mr. M. and this is his account:

"I was called by the sergeant on duty of the Police Station at ****** to go to the P. village. At about 4 am we were already on our way back on a route that led us through fields and forests. At some point my partner felt a degree of anxiety and was apparently nervous for some reason. She said that something is about to happen. When we drove out of P*****, we noticed lights in the distance, located somewhere over the forest.

At first it looked like the illumination of the BTS tower but after short discussion we realised that there are no similar installations in that area. After a short while the light disappeared from our sight and then reappeared to left, still staying several miles way in the distance. At first it looked like the moon and was positioned very low over the horizon. It was red, yellow and orange in color. At first we took it for the moon but according to our estimations the moon should have been in another part of the sky. So I decided to stop the car and examine the object more closely. It could be seen even from this distance that the ball of light was getting bigger and then smaller. It also changed shape from circular to semi-circular and was radiating a number of colored lights.

Then it got bigger and we realised that it was not growing in size but was approaching us instead! In stopped over the trees about half a mile away and then I was able to make out the exact shape of the object. It was stationary and soundless. At some point small balls of lights began to break off from its underneath. Some were returning into it while others just disappeared in mid air. After this the main object generated a stroboscope-like flash of light that illuminate a vast area.

We both became concerned at this point because nothing like this had ever happened to us before. We jumped into our car and drove away but at the same time the object began moving and began running parallel to us! We stopped again in the next village capturing a short video of the UFO in the distance. For unknown reasons, we felt as if we were in some kind of danger. We made a third stop next to a small parking bay adjacent to some farm buildings.

At that moment the object approached and stayed about a mile from us so we could now make out its solid outline. It was a disc-shaped object topped with a dome, emitting strong, dazzling lights of a yellow color (sometimes changing to orange). On its bottom part three smaller, spherical, light-blue elements could be seen. At first I took it for the UFOs engines but as I said before, they made no noise. Our sighting was short, maybe only a minute in duration.

Because we feared that something might happen to us I soon asked my partner to return to the car. I would like to add that during the sighting our radio *went dead but this is quite normal in that area. We quickly drove off and the object was pacing us, staying at an approximate distance of a mile. We made two more attempts to stop and observe it but every time the object reacted and withdrew. When we passed K*****, it backed off for the last time and disappeared for good.*

Back at our base, I immediately informed the sergeant on duty but he did not believe me and laughed at us. He said that I must be overtired and had hallucinated! Our superiors reacted in the same way, trying to persuade us that we saw balloons or flocks of birds! Although I reported to them the details of the entire sighting it was apparent that they were not about to believe me."

Mr. M.'s partner was not very eager to disclose all the details but she had a number of very important personal reasons not to do so. But that was not the end of the affair. Upon returning to base, the witnesses were interrogated and informed that their case would be relayed to the chief officer. In Mr. M.'s opinion, his superiors were clearly confused by the entire situation. However, this was not the end and something even more controversial came to light. There was a gap in the time-line in the witnesses report. They arrived at the station at about 5:30am, after traveling a distance that according to map is less than 12 miles. At 4:32 they took a video (showing a bright spot in the distance, low over the horizon) and then continued their way. The other important element is that both experienced a strong sense of agitation and anxiety during the sighting.

Mr. M. said that before the first confrontation with the object, shortly after his partner exclaimed her anxiety, he felt dizzy for a moment. His partner complained of dizziness just after their return to the police station.

To this day it is still unknown whether or not they simply lost their way or maybe experienced a missing time episode. There are many elements suggesting a strong consciousness-related effect during the sighting. Unfortunately, no other eyewitnesses to this case has emerged even when the local press picked up on the story (which could be partially explained by fact the location of the sighting is sparsely populated). Mr. M. was at first was afraid of the consequences of revealing his experience to the media but his doubts were quickly swept under the rug by his superiors who classified the events as the misidentification of lights in the distance. An unexpected result of this was that fellow officers began contact him, sharing their own stories of sighting of unidentified objects. One of them, who then forwarded his story to me, claimed to have observed a row of spherical, red objects hovering in the sky that began to disappear when he tried to approach them in his patrol car.

Did the two police officers experience something far deeper than just a flying saucer sighting? The main witness finds it hard to answer this question. For him it is quite possible that on the night of the encounter something went wrong with his consciousness. Or maybe their sense of time was disrupted by a common fear?

QUOTATION SOURCES

Piotr Cielebiaś and Michał Kuśnierz Archives / *infra.org.pl*

Chapter 16

FORGOTTEN CRASHES & THE JERZMANOWICE EVENT

UFO crash with Hitler in the background • 1st Gdynia event. Crash-landing from 1943 • Węgorzewo crash and military retrieval
Jerzmanowice anomalous event

ONLY few abroad are aware of the fact that the Gdynia event was not the only one alleged UFO crash on Polish territory and according to some it was even the third in ascending order and the second one in the Gdynia area. In this chapter I reexamine these stories and look at some other alleged crashes with the Jerzmanowice event (1993) as the most reliable and mysterious of them all. Although (as it will turn out) it was a non-ufological incident but rather a catastrophe of some *unknown body*, it embraced many phenomena of an anomalous nature.

We should remember that the Gdynia crash of 1959 was a real event though not one that our fellow ufologists considers it the Polish equivalent of the Roswell Incident of 1947. The incident was presumably caused by some sort of space object (early satellite or rocket) while the part of the story involving a humanoid entity came from doubtful foreign sources. But only few realise that the Gdynia crash was preceded by another crash-landing that took place in the city area and was witnessed by a French prisoner of war and was discussed in Jean Sider's book *Ultra Top Secret*.

The 21-year old butcher S. Theau (pseudonym) from the Le Mans area of France in 1943 was imprisoned in the German labour camp in Gdynia where he worked on the construction of bunkers but was then was reassigned to work for a local butcher's shop which was run by a German soldier's wife. Unfortunately *Exelroud* or *Hexelroud* town where it was allegedly located did not exist so it has cast some doubts on the report's reliability. According to French researcher Jean Sider who deemed the witness reliable though simple, Theau was allowed by the camp commendatory to walk freely (Germans must trust him so much!) and in the morning of July 18th, he was walking to work as usual along a sandy bank of Baltic Sea. Walking along the dunes, the Frenchman noticed a flat metallic object partially embedded in the sand. A human figure stood beside it and was apparently trying to dig it up. Suddenly, as if sensing Theau's presence, she turned in his direction revealing her strange appearance. In his opinion she looked almost like a normal woman but her face bore some Asian features. She was 5ft 10 inches tall (more than Theau) long blonde hair and was dressed in a seamless tight-fitting overall without any insignia or markings.

The witness took her for the famous Luftwaffe female pilot, Hanna Reitsch and helped her to dig her experimental craft out of the sand. The object was about 20 ft in diameter and looked like two metallic saucers put together with two rings on their surfaces. It was devoid of any bolts, openings or welds and had several square-like windows on its upper section.

When they managed to get the object out, the space woman who talked in some sort of unintelligible language, touched the Frenchmen's chest with the outer part of her palm, then repeated the gesture on her chest and pointed to the sky. It was a sign that she was about to take off. Then she touched her belt and a door in the object opened. She crawled inside on all fours, the door closed; the saucer rose up and then departed at a tremendous speed.

Chivalrous Theau returned to his duties and some decades later decided to reveal his story, realising that Hanna Reitsch might be in fact an extraterrestrial visitor... Irrespective of the story coherence, its reliability is also decreased by non-existing places indicated by witness.

Far less is known about the source of the much more popular myth of an alleged UFO crash in Czernica (then Langenau) in 1937 when it was a part of the German Third Reich. Versions of this story vary but all declare that on a summer's day an unidentified flying object dropped from the sky into a field belonging to Eva Braun's (Hitler's wife) family and was retrieved by German soldiers. Browsing Internet sources and ufological books of dubious reliability, one can even learn about the object (a *multicolored ball*), its passengers' appearance and their further destiny in Werner von Braun's laboratory. In short, that story is utter rubbish and has never been treated seriously by any Polish researchers. For example in 1945 the Langenau estate was von Klitzing's family property (Eva Braun's family was from München and her father was a teacher, not a landowner). In Robert Leśniakiewicz's opinion, none of Czernica's inhabitants has ever heard about any UFO crash. In my opinion there are two possibilities: either the myth is based on some real experimental airplane crash in 1937 or it is one of the many trash stories on the *Third Reich's flying saucers* that emerged in the tabloid press after the Second World War.

Legends concerning *Die Wunderwaffe* (Hitler's *wonder weapon*) and treasures buried by Germans in the Owl Mountains still haunt Polish Sudetes – one of the most enigmatic regions in the country. Even today stories about mysterious, civilian *keepers* guarding some locations in the area circulate. What they try to keep secret and who pays them remains a mystery bigger than Hitler's flying saucers.

Węgorzewo UFO crash-retrieval

An alleged UFO incident comes from the Węgorzewo area (warmińsko-mazurskie), although sensational, it remains widely unknown, even amongst Polish UFO enthusiasts. After a noisy beginning, it was overwhelmed by understatements and controversy. It all began with reports from the *Gazeta Olsztyńska* (*Olsztyn Newspaper*) disclosing that in March 1997 military exercises in that area were suddenly disturbed by unexpected emergency.

> "At about 5:30pm two soldiers saw a large band of fire coming from south to north and evidently heading towards the ground. This most unusual phenomenon disappeared after about a minute. Soon a deafening 'boom' could be heard amongst the trees. A meteorite impact? Suddenly a radio message was received: Go to the crash-landing location. Do not touch anything. Secure military aircraft crash area" – the article stated, mentioning an alleged informer who then shared his knowledge with UFO researcher Bronisław Rzepecki.

In *Czas UFO* (*UFO Times*) the researcher a much more detailed report on the incident:

> "In early March 1997, two platoons of the 1st Reconnaissance Company of 1st Special Regiment were sent to Orzysze for exercises involving shooting, parachuting and survival skills. On March 14th one of the platoons (21 soldiers + commander) had been transported by an MI-8 helicopter 11 miles north of Węgorzewo, to a forested area dotted with small lakes" – Rzepecki wrote.

The events of March 15th went exactly as it was described in the newspaper. Soldiers soon identified the location of the crash which was deep in the woods, nearly 4 miles from the Russian border. What they saw upon arrival in the area totally shocked them.

> "In a small pond, maybe 60ft across, there was a UFO craft partially stuck in southern bank of the pond (it was strange because soldiers saw it flying

northward so it should have been on the opposite side). Part of the object that was submerged in water was illuminated by a yellowish glow" – Rzepecki wrote.

The soldier's also saw a kind of *mechanic arm* ending with a vertical egg-like structure giving off a pale light. The UFO was about 15 ft in diameter, flattened and in light-silver in color. Soon the soldiers were ordered to encircle the machine with arms at the ready (though equipped only with blanks) and in that formation they waited until 0:30 am when helicopters brought special units and some *high ranking officers*.

And if that's not enough, the damaged object the attempted to defend itself:

"Newcomers surrounded the object. There were also some civilians with a number of caskets. At the same moment the egg suddenly changed color to bluish and an explosion of strong, flash-like light appeared apparently hurting the soldiers in its direct vicinity" – wrote Rzepecki, citing his informer's account.

Probably that was not the end but Rzepecki decided not to disclose any further details. This controversial report spurred many questions, not only concerning its reliability and credibility but also the alleged military procedures. For example why were un-armed soldiers ordered to wait for hours for the special unit's arrival, when instead they could have obtained assistance from the nearby Orzysz base? Maybe the incident was some sort of special military exercise or maybe it was a cover story made for ufologists?

Rzepecki was aware of these possibilities and did not pass sentence on the case but it seemed so far-fetched that even sensation-seeking newspapers gave up on it in the end. But it was not the only case of this kind in Polish ufological annals.

In May 2012 another sensational story emerged, this time involving an alleged barrel-shaped UFO that crashed in the Kampinos Forest – a large forest complex in the Warsaw area and part of the primordial wilderness that once covered that part of Poland. Right from the start it was perfectly obvious that the case was less than credible. An *anonymous informer* from Leoncin village wrote on a number of internet forums that soldiers cordoned off the village looking for debris of an unidentified craft that had disintegrated in the air. The story then went wild and was even picked up by local web portal. Unfortunately it was a total hoax of unknown purpose. It was not long before I came into possession of photographs depicting the alleged debris. The author's and perpetuator's of the entire hoax were either of a young age or a low intellectual level. The alleged evidence included close-up photos of a can and bits of burnt universal cables and wires. A simple hoax soon exposed for being exactly what it was.

Jerzmanowice event

This incident is the only one undoubtedly real anomalous event of the whole group. However on the other hand it perhaps cannot be described as rightful UFO-crash case as you will see. On January 14th 1993, at about 7pm. part of a huge limestone rock called Babia Skała (lit. Old-Woman's Rock) was shattered and its white debris covered the area around it as a result. Witnesses detailed that some pieces of debris were *as big as a bucket* plunging through house roofs and breaking window panes. A short while before this the village was shaken by two loud bangs and a bright flash. Electricity went down and panicked people flocked outside fearing that a gas explosion had occurred. But those who lived in close vicinity to Babia Skała witnessed much more strange phenomena. According to estimates, in more than 30 households electric and electronic utensils (home appliances, TV sets, video players etc.) were damaged and in others electrical wires melted.

Prof. Andrzej Manecki from the Mineralogical and Geochemical Institute of AGH University of Science and Technology in Kraków, who also witnessed the sighting from a distance, wrote in *Meteorite bulletin* (#5/1993) that just before the blast several locals saw a *bluish object* in the air accompanied by a *very dark cloud*. Other reported seeing two objects bouncing off the shattered rock face. Manecki who supervised the research, to his huge surprise, found no traces of meteoritic matter or crater.

Physical and chemical analyses also detected no evidence of cosmic dust or high temperature. The working hypothesis was that the Jerzmanowice area was struck by a *super-bolt (lightning)* accompanied by *ball-lighting* of an intensified force. But to some this theory sounded a bit too fanciful. It surely must be a very rare kind of atmospheric anomaly or some military induced incident.

The mystery deepened when Dr. Tomasz Ściężor stated that according to eyewitnesses, at first they heard a humming noise and then the sky turned a bluish color. Then the brilliant object appeared and flew toward Babia Góra and collided with the rock.

Some witnessed reported not only electrical disturbances but also St. Elmo's fire dancing on the tops of metal items and even domestic utensils levitated! The blast and fall of debris was followed by short hail storm with a strong wind. Then a chemical smell permeated the area, similar to the odor of chemical fertiliser and a thin gray smoke appeared near Babia Skała. Late that night a group of soldiers appeared and cordoned off the area of the explosion but they found nothing unusual. Locals who reached the rock just before the soldiers also did not notice anything out of ordinary. The village's inhabitants were obviously shaken and flabbergasted and no one was able to explain the event. Fortunately there were no casualties but what would have happened if the object had smashed into the Jerzmanowice houses?

The incident of 1993 illustrates well the politics of the Polish authorities is response to an event that is beyond their realm of control. If no one was injured, who cares about the answers?

The Jerzmanowice event was similar to another explosion but probably of smaller intensity that in 1978 had shaken the Bickford farm of Bell Island (Canada). But in my archive I have also some other cases of similar characteristics but again featuring less powerful explosions. For example, in 1986 a dark cloud appeared over the energy distribution center near Częstochowa (in the same Jura region as Jerzmanowice). In broad daylight a powerful explosion occurred (without any observable objects) and some people were knocked off of their feet by the blast wave it generated.

It is well known that the Jerzmanowice explosion was witnessed from Cracow located just 12 miles away. One academician who witnessed the event from Cracow Old Town said that he thought that it was an "atomic explosion" (that illustrates what people from under Babia Skała must have experienced). The blast was also registered by seismic stations and observed by the flight controller from Balice but the Army refused to disclose any further details. Was the explosion the result of a stray weapon test involving electromagnetic effects or rather some rare but powerful natural effect? Unfortunately, the answer remains unresolved and is bolstered by mundane explanations from both the Polish military and scientists.

By coincidence the Jerzmanowice event went largely unreported in the national media as at the same time the tragic sinking of the Polish ferry *Jan Heweliusz* took place at about 4 am on January 14th in the western part of Baltic Sea and cost the lives of 55 people.

QUOTATION SOURCES

Piotr Cielebiaś and Michał Kuśnierz Archives / *infra.org.pl*

WMGU Archives

Rzepecki B., *Kolejna katastrofa UFO w Polsce*, Czas UFO, #2/1998.

Rzepecki B., *Bliskie spotkania z UFO w Polsce*, Tarnów 1995.

Lądowisko pod Węgorzewem, Gazeta Olsztyńska, 14-16/10/1997.

Manecki A., *Interesujące zjawisko w Jerzmanowicach z dnia 13 stycznia 1993*, Meteoryt, March 1993.

Chapter 17

USOs & UFOs OVER THE BALTIC SEA

**USO in Baltic Sea • Ball just over the surface • Fishermen paralysed by UFO
Boat master lost his sight during UFO contact • Piaski video**

FOR thousands of Polish people the Baltic Sea is a traditional holiday destination in both the summer and the winter. The Baltic is strongly connected with Polish tradition and history. In ancient Slavonic times it was populated by Pomeranian tribes whose descendants, Kashubians, still use a language that sounds weird for other Poles. In the West few are aware of the fact that every region of our country has its own identity, dialect, traditions and lifestyle. Some are more conservative, other secular, in other parts Russian influences can be seen and of course German in others. This fascinating mosaic paints a real picture of Poland, a country still balancing between West and East.

I previously mentioned a number of reports of UFO sightings that took place near the Baltic shores, such as the Gdynia crash (1959), Hel humanoids (1981) or Wicie photos (1983). In Polish ufologists' archives there are many more spectacular instances involving both sightings of UFOs over the surface of the sea as well as rare encounters with mysterious USOs (acronym for unidentified submersible objects). One of the few Polish reports of objects qualifying as a USO sighting was described by Arek Miazga. In 2001 dozens of passengers onboard the Rogalin ferry (one of many regularly cruising to Denmark, Sweden, Germany etc.) witnessed an object that was 10 ft diameter that came up to the sea's surface about 165 yards from the vessel:

"There were around 40 people onboard and all watched the event. Many of my acquaintances, who were skeptical and ignorant, could not believe what they had reported. All the witnesses were astounded when they realised that

the object they previously took to be a buoy, suddenly at a tremendous speed approached the vessel, submerged and maneuvered under water. After three minutes it stopped and we sailed away, leaving it behind."

Another interesting observation of a group of objects was submitted to Arek Miazga by a ferry passenger who in June or July 1997 was sailing to Stockholm. The Baltic waters became dull and twilight was fast approaching. Standing on the upper deck and admiring the panorama, the man decided to return to his cabin to put on something warm because he was about to continue his sightseeing up on deck.

"I then returned to the upper deck, opened the door and then, exactly in front of me a big ball became visible, being very low over the sea's surface. It was a sphere about 30 ft cross and had a completely flat surface. Its color resembled lava or molten metal. I would say that it was a kind of stationary plasma sphere. It was did not move but the colors inside the object were in constant motion. Immediately I thought: 'I should go and get my camera.' But it would take me several minutes to do so. So at first I decided to examine the object from the closest possible distance. After a short while from upper part of the object some smaller spheres emerged and stayed in 10 ft range from the mother object. There were up to 10 of them. I could clearly see the way they separated off. Their glow did not irritate my eyes. On the surface of the big ball (or beneath it) some darker colored spots were rotating."

The witness who was 19 years old at the time, tried to look for other potential observers. All the passengers were inside apart from two Swedes who were evidently *under the influence of alcohol but* who did catch a glimpse of the UFO and commented on it to one another. From the departing ferry the unusual phenomenon was visible for several minutes and then the lights just went off.

Fishermen's weird encounter

Another most unusual Baltic Sea encounter took place in August 1979 and involved the crew of two fishing boats which met with an official response from the Polish Navy and featured in the mainstream press (as *Polityka* – one of the main opinion-forming newspapers). The reason behind such interest was that the UFO sighting resulted in unexplained and potentially dangerous after effects on the witnesses' that required emergency medical intervention.

The incident involved two modern boats belonging to the Szomborg family that on August 23rd 1979. 29-year-old Lucjan Szomborg – master of Hel-127 boat, at about 3 pm received directions from his father concerning fishing in the high sea's they were about to reach. The journey lasted for several hours. The first unexpected problems of a technical nature began at about 7:30 when Henryk

Elwardt who navigated the ship noticed that the radar had broken down. The radar then inexplicably returned to normal functioning but then again about 20:15 it went haywire again along with the ship's TV set.

> "At the same time, in the darkening sky, Lucjan Szomborg noticed two bright-red lights less than a mile from ship's starboard. He took them for helicopters that in Elwardt's opinion were just one-third of a mile away but all were confused with lack of any sounds" – Rzepecki and Piechota wrote.

> "The master of the ship was about to observe it with binoculars but suddenly both object's began to move toward another ball of light, much bigger than them and pulsating with light, that appeared in the distance. The witnesses got the impression that the pair of bright-red spheres formed in fact parts of a single object. Then all the objects disappeared in the distance but according to mechanic Andrzej Ustrabowski, a white sphere emerged and began to hover in the mid-air at the same level as the pulsating one."

The ball hovering over the Baltic began to emit dazzling pulses of light that fascinated Szomborg so much that he decided to approach the object. When the boat changed course, it turned out that the UFO also moved and stopped on a collision course. After a third attempt, the master felt the first strike of a strange energy. He said that it started from his legs that weakened and his chest area seemed heavier. He also could smell a nauseating, sweet odor resembling that of snuff. An atmosphere of curiosity amongst the crewmen turned into horror when the same affliction gripped Elwardt.

> "He stiffened and released the steering wheel. Leaning over the door of the master's cabin he looked frozen and pale. Fighting with pain, Szomborg managed to enter the small ship's bridge and changed course. He noticed that the compass did not work. Suddenly he realised that his father's boat is somewhere in the vicinity and he decided to warn him about the dangerous object" – the two researchers wrote.

Augustyn Szomborg at first reprimanded his son for things they did with the boat but acknowledged that he could see through his binoculars a red ball emitting light that reflected off of the water's surface. Meanwhile on Hel-127, two other fishermen, Paweł Bona and Janusz Figurski, felt unwell after viewing the strange object. One of them complained of a *tightening band around his head*. When Szomborg found them kneeling and holding their heads, he directed them to go under the deck where the most solid part of ship would perhaps provide added protection from the illness-inducing *energy* evidently coming from the pulsating object.

Szomborg stayed on the bridge and feeling barely alive tried to navigate the boat and free it from the object's influence. The task turned into a nightmare:

"He could feel the symptoms of paralysis coming over him and at the same moment he entered into seconds long bouts of blindness as well. He said that the air around him rhythmically pulsated. He alternately lost and regained consciousness" – Rzepecki and Piechota mentioned adding that Bona who hid with others under the deck, sneezed for a quarter of an hour and could not control it!

After about 20 minutes, Szomborg noticed that the sphere was no longer following the boat and lay behind them in the distance. The master regained his sight and they safely returned to Hel port at 4am. Their vessel immediately underwent radiation tests but the result was negative. All the onboard equipment was working fine. What is interesting however is that during the encounter, despite the crew being affected by the strange energy force, the ship's engine worked normally. This of course raised many questions concerning the type of influence and effect that was generated by the sphere.

All the fishermen were examined by doctors, neurologists and psychiatrists with no aberrations found though they were prescribed sedatives and were not allowed back out to sea for three weeks. Why did the Polish Navy react in such a way by not allowing these men back out to sea for three weeks? Unfortunately the answer to this question remains unknown as the results of the analysis and investigation by the Polish Navy has never been made available. Officially no military activities were taking part in the area where the sighting was made. There was one theory that the crew had fallen victim of a can of toxic gas. During and after WWII mostly German (but also Soviet) forces sank masses of toxic gases in the Baltic.

Only now have they acknowledged that it is a real problem but there has been no clean up of this mess by the Polish authorities. But if the Hell-127 fishermen were poisoned by toxic gases, some of them surely would die or suffer serious aftereffects (reports mention only temporary trauma). The gas theory also does not explain the apparently intelligently controlled UFOs appearance. Without a doubt, this incident from 1979 remains one of the most fascinating and mysterious events described in this book.

UFOs have often invaded the Baltic Sea shore. From another incident it is perhaps worth mentioning the yellow, ellipsoidal object sighting by a pair of scouts on night duty in August 1982. They claimed to approach the object that then shot off while making 'metallic' sounds. What is interesting is that the young witnesses claimed to find a hot spot of sand and a smoldering *piece of* driftwood in the area where the object was observed. Just before the object's disappearance they also – according to the main witness, Joanna, felt some kind of psychical influence preventing them from getting any closer.

Yet another very interesting case from Piaski took place on August 20th 2003 in Vistula Spit – the peninsular stretch of land bisected by the Polish-Russian border. On the date in question Mr. Frank Delephine – a Frenchman who was visiting the Piaski resort, took a video of some strange objects that still can be found on YouTube. For the spectators on the beach the sight must have been spectacular. There was a group of yellowish lights in formation resembling the number five on a dice. Some of the lights were evidently in motion which is clearly visible in final part of the video. Delephine related that the objects were leaving a smoke trail. The Cometa group that investigated the sighting deemed it impossible to explain but there might possibly be a military operation that could explain it.

Piaski is located at the tip of the Vistula Spit. On the opposite side there is Baltiysk – a major naval base of the Baltic Fleet. It must be also noted that identical objects were seen and photographed in 1991 over Greifswald in Germany. To this day that sighting has no definite explanation.

UFO sightings over Polish seas also feature cases of high strangeness. For example, in 2008 I was contacted by a former journalist (now living in the UK) who reported to me a very strange adventure on a Baltic beach, in the already mentioned Wicie area, on the night of July 13th 2006. During her summer walks on the beach she decided to spend a night at the beach with her dog. Finding a comfortable place, she listened intently sounds of the sea. But about 11 pm she noticed something strange that scared her so much that she hid in the nearby forest. She said that up to 10 ft above the water she noticed a number of maneuvering lights which were red and blue in color. At first she tried to explain the sight in conventional terms but surely they were no people around with flashlights.

> *"Then I began to look around wondering if there were any big ships in the area. I examined the scenery and noticed a huge glow with twinkling lights inside"* – she said.

> *"As it turned out, the glow surrounded a huge saucer-shaped object of a gray-metallic structure that hovered just over the sea not too far from the shore. It was of gargantuan dimensions and had lights turning on alternately from left to right."*

But after this point in her sighting her conscious memories become quite hazy. She could only remember that the sea was roaring louder than usual, her cell phone went crazy and she woke up in strange mood. Did the object in the distance influence her as it was with Szemborg's crew or maybe it was just a dream?

QUOTATION SOURCES

Piotr Cielebiaś and Michał Kuśnierz Archives / *infra.org.pl*

Arek Miazga Archive / arekmiazga.blogspot.com

Piechota K., Rzepecki B., *UFO nad Polską*, Białystok 1996.

Chapter 18

UFO ABDUCTIONS IN POLAND

**Controversial bedroom visitations • Mother and daughter experiences
Szczecin terrifying experience • Abduction and intelligence boost
Zofia Namlik's case**

STORIES concerning people being allegedly abducted by aliens seem the most vibrant and sensational part of the UFO phenomenon but equally the most problematic. It is hard to crack the mystery of experiences that take place both on both a physical level and on another plane of reality. Whoever the cosmic kidnappers are, they possess the ability to completely control the witness' will, its environment and the laws of space-time as well. Aware of the complex nature of the phenomenon, some researchers tend to classify alien abductions as either *spiritual* or paranormal in origin rather than extraterrestrial.

As an inherent part of UFO-lore and pop-culture, alien abductions tend to be lumped together with bedroom visitations, sleep paralysis and hypnagogia/hypnopompia experiences. All of them involve grotesque visions and terrifying sensations but some can be explained in medical neurological terms. One must bear this fact in mind when reading that a high percentage of people believe that they have undergone an alien abduction experience (Apelle estimated it could be up to 5 percent of the global population). Certainly a substantial part of them stem from experiences that despite being traumatic and frightening could well be explained.

There are still two unanswered questions basic to abduction experiences that may reveal a great deal on the nature and origin of the alien abduction phenomenon. The first problem concerns its global distribution, second, the cultural distribution. We simply don't know whether the phenomenon is uniform all over the world, or it varies according to culture. Scenario's involving Gray aliens and bright medical rooms, popularised with Budd Hopkins' books, is not so common outside of the United States. So what does the alien abduction phenomenon really look like in Poland?

Controversial bedroom visitations

Polish UFO researchers have come across abduction stories only occasionally. In fact only a few such *cases* are taken seriously in Poland. They either do not occur or witnesses prefer not to report them out of fear and ridicule. Much more frequent are stories involving the typical bedroom visitation scenario. The witness woke up at night feeling eerie atmosphere. Everything around the room looks fine but there is a menacing presence or sensation of being stared at. Then usually some sort of strange entity enters or appears. For unknown reasons, the beings that appear during these incidences are usually described as being dark and hooded figures.

Although similar experiences left people in state of shock (especially those who experienced it for the first time), they came from a vast reservoir of neurological effects known as hypnagogia – an onset to dreaming, when one's brain is transiting from one state to another. Hypnagogia embrace's a broad set of experiences such as: hearing sudden voices or screams, seeing of kaleidoscopic images, weird luminosity, temporarily paralysis and much more. "Dictionary of Hallucinations" also counts other hypnagogia hallucinatory motifs (according to Andreas Mavromatis) as "formless, designs, faces, figures, animals, objects, and nature scenes, scenes with people, print and writing". Gamers often see game scenes when they close eyes. This is also a form of hypnagogia. (The same effects but before waking up are called hypnopompia.)

Interpretations vary according to the witness who could take them as visions, out-of-body-experiences or even close encounters. A typical hypnagogical bedroom visitation occurred to a young man, Kamil B. from the Częstochowa area who in 2008 went to sleep but woke up a while after hearing two male screams. Suddenly he found himself unable to move but managed to open an eye. Shaken and terrified, he saw a dark hooded, dwarfish entity that floated across the room. He then fully woke up and was so terrified that for several nights he slept with light on. When presented with the hypnagogic hypothesis he stated that the strange hallucination could be induced by the fact that on the night of the experience he fell asleep with headphones on listening to music.

But there are controversial hypnagogies too and both examples also come from Częstochowa area. The first involves a young man who in the summer of 1996 had a vision of a strange creature after waking up during the night and seeing a strange,

5 ft tall being who stood against the window, partially enveloped in moonlight.

> "An absolute silence fell. It then smiled at me but its grin was kind of ironical. I was scared. I started to call my mum who slept in her room but with no results. So I ran to her and tried frantically to wake her up. But she was in some kind of stupor" – he related. "When I looked at the clock in my parents' room it was about 1:30 am. The strangest thing is that I don't know to this day how I returned to my bed. When I woke up again it was about 4 am."

Details of his experience are unlike the transitional and quick nature of hypnagogia. As he said, in the first phase of the encounter his mind had seemingly gone out of control and despite his panic, the witness approached the night intruder noticing its wrinkled, clay-like facial skin and the shining cloth wrapping its body. It is also interesting that in the morning he noticed a number of scratches and reddened skin on his mother's cheeks – evidence of the night time experience?

In late January 2011 a 39-year-old woman from Żarki Letnisko (also in Częstochowa area) related to me her strange story.

> "On that day along with my husband we went to work and everything was normal. Then we returned home to our village. That evening was calm. My husband was awake but I went to sleep at around 10.30 pm. Suddenly I was awoken by some kind of inner sensation similar to that of being stared at. So I opened my eyes and saw (it is hard to find the appropriate words) a kind of sphere. For me it looked like the pupil of an eye. The light it emitted was not dazzling. Inside of the object I saw two black dots. For several seconds it hovered in the mid-air, then became fainter and slowly floated away towards the window and dwindled away! I was lying motionless, paralysed by strange sensation that I could not understand. Moreover, during the encounter I had a picture of some stony area engraved in my mind. In the morning I was still lightheaded. I can't believe in all this… Two weeks have passed and I am still looking around, fearing that the thing would return."

It would seem that this experience was the result of either hypnagogia or possibly something of a paranormal origin? It seems that the border between bedroom visitations, sleep-related hallucinations, spiritual experiences and alien abductions is very thin. This can be seen in cases similar to that of Małgorzata Jeleńska and her daughter from Bydgoszcz in north-western Poland.

Their story was reported by Wojciech Chudziński – my friend and in my opinion the best Polish writer dealing with paranormal phenomena. In 2003 he published a collection of reports making a unique book about paranormal experiences of the average Polish citizen. One of them concerned the experiences of a 41-year-old woman – a cloakroom attendant in one of the high-schools in Bydgoszcz who claimed to have been X-rayed by alien humanoids during a bedroom visitation. It was preceded by a series of loud sounds of unidentified origins that haunted their flat.

> "I heard a loud banging, similar to that when the big garbage truck is passing by our window. I looked out of the window afraid that some airplane crash was going to happen but the street was calm and empty. Then the noise reappeared and it was hard to withstand. Added to this a bright piercing light appeared that illuminated the building across the street" – she said.

Panicked, she rushed to her daughter's cot but soon the sound was gone. Mr. Małgorzata noticed only some sparks falling in front of the window which quickly disappeared. The skeptical woman treated this as a kind of hallucination being unable to explain why her husband, older daughter and neighbors from the apartment house witnessed nothing. In her opinion the strange event was a precursor to the night visitation that took place two weeks later.

> "I woke up at night seeing two human-like beings in the room. They looked at my younger daughter's cot and at the same time I received a communication in my mind: 'She's too young'. After a short while I found myself in a kind of void with Ania – my older daughter. I held her hand. I saw the pair of aliens and a third woman-like being who accompanied them. I then received another calming communication telling me not be afraid because they only want to X-ray us" – she reported. (In fact the intruders didn't use the X-ray term. In Polish it's called prześwietlenie, i.e. penetration by light.)

> "They assured me that I would not be touched and held their apparatus at a distance. I remember being terribly cold. I was shaking. At some point Ania disappeared from my sight and I found myself under something akin to a shower. They informed me that it was a kind of purification after the procedure. Then everything went black. After a while I awoke in my bed with my husband sleeping at my side. At this point the roaring noise reappeared."

Mr. Mirosław Jeleński – the witness's husband – could also hear it and said it was different to that made by an airplane. He added that his wife was all shaking despite the hot summer night.

> "When I was taken by them, I admired their bodies. They allowed me to touch them" – Mrs. Małgorzata related.

> "For me they looked identical to humans but they were so soft, as if stuffed with cotton wool. And their skin was exceptionally bright with the color of the white inside a boiled egg. The man was tall and blonde, with short hair."

An experience of similar origin involved Witold Rusek in the late PRP era. The inhabitant of Warsaw claimed that when he turned off the radio playing rock music, he looked out of the window and saw a brilliant object. Momentarily he could see the wall opening and 7ft tall beings in white robes emerging. He said that they stood on something resembling ramp of light that soon got closer to the couch the man was sitting on and touched his arm above the wrist. Rusek claims that he then experienced an OBE experience flew out with them from the apartment into the object where he was subjected to a medical examination. He liked the milky-white interior of the UFO craft so much that he asked one of the beings if he could stay with them.

"No time for such deeds" – the alien replied.

Experiences of non-sleeping minds

In the section detailing the St. Ann's Hill encounters I mentioned a kind of UFO-mania that affected the main witness, Grzegorz Nowak. But something of a much stronger and frightening nature occurred to a middle-aged couple from Szczecin in 1986. The experience that started with a bedroom visitation resulted in an episode where the female witness' consciousness interception triggered a wide range of unconventional behaviors. It took place on the evening of April 23rd (Wednesday) in the small flat of Marian and Czesława G. on Gdyńska Street.

Rzepecki and Piechota wrote that Mrs. Czesława woke up hearing the sounds of the TV Daily News (Dziennik Telewizyjny) but noticed momentarily that the TV screen went black (with TV still on). At the same moment she noticed two beings standing just 3 ft away from the couch. Concerned, she shouted at her husband: "Have you let any strangers in?"

The man woke up and was amazed at the sight and stated that he had not let anyone in. There were two silhouettes standing in the middle of the room. No facial features were recognisable – their heads seemed to be made of a white mass while their torsos – in the opinion of Mr. Czesława – were greenish and similar to military uniforms. Moreover, the pair did not remember seeing the intruders' arms. Then, in some unexplained manner, both beings changed positions and sat by them. Though the beings had no eyes, the woman said she could feel their stare. At that moment she received the following communication in her head:

"We need you for human reproduction. The calendar will change. We are otherworldly beings."

For reasons unknown to her, she decided to go with them! At that moment both beings disappeared in plain sight. The witnesses stood up and noticed that their TV set was still broken. Suddenly they noticed a brilliant object attempting to land on a nearby hill where a small park was located. When the light landed it began to radiate strong beams of light in the direction of the witness's apartment window, (it is interesting that in Czesława G.'s opinion the object was red but Mr. Marian described it as blue). Remembering the alien's proposal and the landed object looked like the UFO from the earlier incident, the nearly hypnotised woman said: *"I'm going with them."*

Then she described the urge as being caused by *"some waves flowing in my mind. It was as if my brain was going to explode"*. Fortunately, her husband caught her but then was thrown to the floor by some unseen force pressing him to the ground. He was able to get up and the restored the woman's senses had returned to normal. Soon both returned home. Unable to explain the nature of the bright object that was standing on the ground just 45 yards away from their flat, they decided to ask neighbors if they could see it. But they could not! The area was empty. It is worth noting that the hill in question was not directly accessible and separated by wire a fence.

To Mr. Marian's growing fright and consternation, his wife was again possessed by a strange force. Rzepecki and Piechota wrote that she was standing in the window, staring at the object and grasping the net curtain so close that she broke pulled it down. When her husband tried to lay her on the couch with her head turned towards the wall (to avoid the influence of beams), he was struck with the strange force for a second time and fainted. He could not see the light when he regained consciousness but his wife could. He quickly went out to check the situation. He jumped over the fence and reached the hill but found nothing. Meanwhile, Mr. Czesława lost consciousness. She managed to come round but found herself lying naked on the floor.

When the woman looked at the red object, it seemed fainter and fainter. Then it apparently changed form and looked like *an eye*. She did not see it disappear and she was trying to recover from her experience. Researchers who were contacted by the couple just after the strange experience said the only contradicting element of their story was the color of the sphere. Surely the case of Czesława and Marian G. would be deemed as an attempted abduction in which something might have gone wrong. What would have happened if the woman had reached the object remains open to question.

Nearly six months after the Szczecin incident another encounter occurred that began a long series of experiences for Zofia Namlik. The case gained some popularity in the 1990s and was covered several times in the national media. She claimed that her controversial claims were corroborated by medical test results that revealed a strange object in her brain tissue that in the doctors' opinion could not get there in any conventional way.

The story began in October 1986 when the Namliks went on mushroom-picking trip in the Wolsztyn area (western Poland). The pair walked in the forest and at some moment heard a sound resembling a chainsaw engine at work but they did not pay much attention to it. Mr. Zofia separated and went to pick mushrooms and it was at this point that she was startled to see a strange figure approaching her at pace. Having no time to react, she was soon confronted by a humanoid entity in a grey suit with pitch-black eyes. It quickly held up it hands exposing hypnotizing "dark circles with pulsating centers" positioned just below the wrists. Namlik, realising that she was loosing her sight, with a huge effort she managed to scream her husband's name who later claimed that upon arriving at the location, he observed the strange figure quickly moving away. Although Mrs. Zofia soon came round, her weirdest experiences were about to begin. The family related that in the next few days after the encounter in the trees, all the electronic equipment in their house went crazy.

Before I discuss the rest of her story it must be said that it was Kazimierz Bzowski who reported it and in the mid-1990s and popularised the hypothesis concerning the alleged implant in Namlik's body.

Although Bzowski by some is deemed to be a fair and scrupulous researcher, I can not get rid of the idea that he sensationalised many accounts that appeared in his books and articles. For some unknown reasons he tended to publish stories that would persuade people not interested in ufology that it was really a topic for nuts and weirdoes. His writings teemed with cases of monsters emerging from wells, saucers landing in cabbage-fields and many other sensational stories. Bzowski even claimed that on one occasion he photographed an alien being but being so afraid of it that he destroyed all the evidence.

Such details do not support Bzowski's credibility but we must adhere to the facts. This situation of course brings into question the credibility of Namlik's experience. It is unknown whether it was implanted with some fanciful elements but there is (as you will see) some unexplained twists for us to consider. Let us see what Bzowski wrote concerning her further experiences.

"In 1992, during a trip into the woods, Mrs. Zofia came across a strange object in the form of a silvery cupola. A humanoid emerged out of it and the witness noticed a surgical room and figures dressed as doctors as if preparing for an operation. She then awoke on the path to her house. For several days she could not get out of her mind the feeling that something important happened but she could not remember anything. It was her husband who observed a patch

of missing hair on Mrs. Zofia's scalp. Soon they found barely visible scars from surgical cuts of unknown origin. Namliks' house was also haunted by some invisible guest. Even Zofia's husband and two adult sons could feel its presence and observed it several times for a fraction of second. He looked like a normal, tall man. Zofia also started to receive telepathic communicates informing her that the being is helping her to stay in good condition after the surgery she had been subjected to. Because she complained of some strange sensation in that area, she went to see a neurologist who ordered a brain scan" – Bzowski wrote.

He also cited the brain scan results card dated on May 15th 1995 which stated that: "Number of scan: 4110. Scan discovered in lentiform nucleus and anterior limb of internal capsule areas point in dimensions equal to 2x2x1,2 cm (regular geometrical form suggest it isn't a tissue growth but a foreign object) surrounded with blood. Abscess, tumor or some solid body or even the smallest dimensions would result in patient's death." But Zofia Namlik is well and still alive. She also extended her story to into a saga of UFO abductions. Now she is acting like an energy healer but little more is known about her alleged implants. In 1998 she showed up at a few ufological conventions but then she disappeared from the scene and the media lost interest in her. Later a number of claims appeared that the implant in her head had disappeared under unclear circumstances. It is a pity that the potential of this case was wasted and it remains highly controversial as a result.

In a previous chapter I mentioned *Nieznany Świat* and its huge archive containing reports on paranormal phenomena and unexplained experiences from its readers. In 2013 the magazine published a very long account of 72-year-old Tadeusz Kujda who reported a possible abduction incident from his childhood that strongly influenced his future life. It was about 1950 when along with his parents he lived in Bodzanów village near Głucholazy, just next to the Polish-Czechoslovakian border. It all happened when with two friends he was camping by a local river, in a place located in the vicinity of a local paper mill and just several miles away from the border line.

"On the Biała river bank we lit a small campfire and roasted some potatoes. It became late but none of us had a watch. All of a sudden, somewhere over the chimneys of the paper mill, a small orange-red point became visible. Approaching us it decelerated and stopped a dozen of yards over the river, hovering up to 50 ft above the water's surface" – he reported.

Mr. Kujda remembered that the sphere's color seemed a mixture of orange red but the most original feature was located around the object's perimeter. It was a kind of band of some twisted elements of unknown kind, resembling matter consisting of some distorted light. Whatever it was, the object was soundless and emitted a light strong enough to illuminate the entire area. *"All looked as if it was on fire"* – the witness reported. "I don't know how long we stood and watched the object. Probably at first we weren't scared at all but then we were grasped by sudden panic and fled the area. We hurriedly reached my house when my worried mother, grandma, aunts and my father-in-law awaited. We told them what had just happened to us by the river. My friends were so scared that they slept at my house that night. I can remember that night as very tough night for us all. I felt there was a kind of electric current coming from my head down to toes. I swept profusely. I don't know if any of my friends' had any aftereffects because we have never talked about it. After some time I discovered a red growth on my abdomen, the size comparable to half of my little finger, with rounded ends. It seemed as if made of tough rubber but on the other hand it wasn't painful. At first I took it for some kind of tumor and asked many people what it could be but fortunately it did not turn malignant or anything drastic.

But I was changed by the event to such extent that it was shocking for me. My problems with reading were gone. In just a few days I read all my schoolbooks and had no learning problems which I previously had."

In short, Mr. Kujda is in no doubt that his UFO experience resulted in a kind of intellectual boost but also made personal and spiritual changes to him. But on the other hand it left some negative effects as well. He said that from some unknown reasons he lost navigation and orientation skills and was very afraid of the dark and sleeping alone. He was haunted continuously by the same dream which he would often have several times on the same night.

"It was dark and I was standing amongst reeds or bushes. I could hear a terrible humming noise and some kind of being was approaching. It was screaming and I was afraid of it" – he said.

Kujda, who now lives in Germany, stated that all the frightening thoughts and dreams reappeared when he watched a TV documentary on alien abductions. Determined, he tried to find his old friends in Bodzanów. He found Adam – one of the boys who witnessed the strange incident over Białka. Kujda visited his house and asked him a question about that event but the man shut his door. After some time he found out that Adam had committed suicide.

The now elderly man has been never subjected to regressive hypnosis that could possibly deepen his understanding of the things that happened on that night. Kujda still does not know what happened to him but admits that the experience started in him a moral and mental evolution. As all who have experienced an alien abduction, he would not be the same man without his UFO experience.

QUOTATION SOURCES

Piotr Cielebiaś and Michał Kuśnierz Archives / *infra.org.pl*

Piechota K., Rzepecki B., *UFO nad Polską*, Białystok 1996.

Chudziński W., Oszubski T., *Niewyjaśnione zjawiska w Polsce*, Kraków 2003.

Kujda T., *Piorun kulisty, wzięcie, czy…? Incydent sprzed lat i reszta życia*, Nieznany Świat, 8/2013.

Chapter 19

THE GLINIK ANOMALOUS ZONE

Paralysed by loaf-shaped UFO • Sphere in the chimney • Apparitional cross and pillar over cornfield • Alien or Jesus? • Hovering entities • Village taboo

RUSSIAN literature dealing with the paranormal abounds with reports on "anomalous zones", i.e. places or whole regions where extraordinary events occur on regular basis. The biggest country in the world is literally littered with them. Some zones as legendary as Death Valley on the Vilui River allegedly houses a number of ancient ruins of unknown origin, while others spur legends regarding their negative influence on human beings. There are also a number of locations known for their increased UFO activity like the so called M-Triangle located around Molyebka village or city of Tolyatti known as the Russian UFO center.

Not surprisingly Poland has its own anomalous zones. The first such zone features the most unusual and controversial locality known for its numerous high-strangeness reports involving UFOs and non-human entities. In recent times it has gained popularity due to several publications that led to the area being flooded with paranormal buffs or sensation-seekers.

A chain of unexplained activity in Glinik – a small village located about 18 miles from Rzeszów, was discovered by Arek Miazga who from one of his informants learned of alleged flying (or rather floating) entities encountered by many of the local population. The process of data gathering was tough and long. Only after Arek gained a degree of acceptance in the local farming community did a number of witnesses reluctantly admit that they had witnessed something that could not be described in conventional terms. In Arek's opinion, there are two types of anomalous experiences typical of Glinik. The first involves close encounters with unidentified objects of various shapes (discs, balls and crosses) but usually rather small in size. The second type are close encounters with human-like beings that are able to float in the mid-air but do not have any influence on the witnesses. One of the locals residents who came across such a being on his property, asked with fear in his eyes: "Pardon me mister… Are you Jesus?"

Too strange to talk about

Several years ago Arek found out from his informant in Glinik that he had gathered a few UFO-related stories from local area. The village itself is small and although located not far away from Rzeszów – the local administrative center, it maintained a typically rural character with many of the locals earning their living from agriculture. In his spare time Arek was visiting the area to get some fresh air and interview the locals about the *strange stories* from the area. After obtaining their confidence, he collected several spectacular cases of high-strangeness type incidents that the witnesses had not shared with anyone before. The encounters spanned a period from the 1950's to 2009 and the most interesting stories involved close encounters with mysterious beings seemingly able to hover in the mid-air.

"One of first incidents I came across involved Mr. L. who as a 6-year-old child experienced a close contact with unidentified object" – Arek Miazga says. "Around 1963, while playing in a nearby barn, he was suddenly covered in 'Goosebumps'. Looking around Outside of the barn, he noticed a strange object shaped like a loaf of bread positioned just 12 ft away from him. It was quite small and was graphite-colored. In Mr. L.'s opinion it was only 3 ft in height and a bit more in diameter. He also noticed that the object's hull was covered with irregular 'patches' that were pulsating alternately. The loaf-shaped object was evidently vibrating but without making any sounds. Despite this weird situation, the boy was not frightened and soon approached and touched the object feeling a sudden jump in temperature. Upon touching the object he was temporarily paralysed."

More than four decades after the event Mr. L. could still remember it very clearly. Fortunately, after a while the strange paralysis disappeared and he was able to run home and call his mother. When they returned to the barn the object was gone. But as Arek soon established, it was the second strange experience by the same family members in the very same location.

Mr. Zofia L. – the witness's mother, could still remember her meeting with a strange floating man that took place some time in the 1950's.

"She stated that on the day in question, in broad daylight, when she went out of her hut, she noticed a strange figure standing 20 ft away from her. The being looked like a well-built man nearly 6ft in height who stood with his back to her. The being was not a neighbor or a prankster. After a while she saw that the man, dressed in a brown suit, took a few steps forward, jumped high in to the air and disappeared" – Arek said.

Arek Miazga also came across some very interesting stories concerning bizarre unidentified flying objects observed in the same village. As he said, it was probably in 1963 when three boys saw a small rectangular UFO that was flying at a height of just 20 ft and it meandered amongst some trees on its way. Then in 1985 a local farmer saw a 5ft tall, multicolored cross with wavy contours. This strange object appeared on his property, between his house and the cowshed but it disappeared after a short while. Other members of the family also reported seeing another UFO in 1976. "It was about 6 pm when a boy ran the into house and with agitation in his voice telling his family that 'something strange is going on outside'. At the same moment the people gathered inside noticed a red light that filled the room. Outside they saw a red, spherical object that was moving towards some nearby meadows and the river. It was about 10 ft in diameter and had kind of horizontal bands on its surface. The spectators also related that 'something was whirling right in the center of the object'. After 15 seconds, it literally disappeared in plain sight, transforming itself into an oblong streak of gray-blue smoke…" – Arek said.

In the summer of 2000 a farmer from Glinik noticed in broad daylight an ashen-gray oblong pillar hovering 45 ft over his cornfield. Each time he tried to approach the object it 'turned off' but then reappeared. During another incident in 2002 three young witnesses were startled by a reddish ball of light that shot out from a chimney of an old, unoccupied hut they were passing by. From a distance of about150 ft they observed the object descending and then hovering over the ground. But they became too afraid to go any closer and ran away. UFO sightings in Glinik were overshadowed by a series of much more mysterious events. A group of local residents confessed to Arek Miazga that they had met strange humanoid beings with the apparent ability to float in mid-air. As it was pointed out before, they did not had not shared their experiences with anyone previously and wanted to remain anonymous. For those who think that they invented the whole saga to draw tourists to the area must be aware that down in Glinik they do not like visitors or tourists. If asked by outsiders about their encounters the locals usually brush them off in a polite but firm manner.

Glinik humanoids

The above mentioned encounter of Mr. Zofia L. was one in a series of similar episodes that stretched from the 1990s right through to the first decade of 21st century. The first report in chronological order is to be honest the most controversial one since it is a typical sleep-related experience and it could have no connection with the rest that followed down the years. It was witnessed by Mrs. Krystyna who went to bed at 11 pm and after a short while experienced complete paralysis which coincided with the sighting of a very skinny being standing next to her bed. She tried to scream feeling the intruder's cold hand on her calf. After about two minutes the being disappeared leaving the witness in strong state of shock.

But other Glinik encounters were very different. One of them was witnessed in August 1997 by Mr. Z. who late at night was on his way to Broniszów – a village just north of Glinik. Admiring the calm and warm night he was unexpectedly confronted by a strange being coming in the opposite direction.

"The walking man suddenly noticed around 150ft away a strange silhouette looking as if it was made of woven light. It was about 5 ft tall but other details could not be distinguished. He only said that the beings head was disproportionate. The man was so scared by that he ran away, falling in to water filled ditch as he did so. When he managed to got out of the ditch the being was gone" – Arek wrote.

The most original of the Glinik encounters took place a year or two later. A simple local man, Mr. Jacek (then about 50 years of age) at about 11 pm noticed a number of bursts of light on his yard. He decided to take a closer look and when he came out he realised that just 90 ft away, beyond a grove of trees was a glowing person could be seen. The figure inside this glow looked dark in color. Mr. Jacek approached it thinking that it could be some kind of teenage prank. "When he stopped just several yards from the thing all his hair stood on end" – Arek wrote.

"The entity was about 6ft tall and wore a long dark cloak. At first sight it looked like a young, short-haired man generating a luminosity of unknown source. But the most intriguing aspect of this event was that Mr. Jacek tried to communicate with the being. He said that at first the man said to him: 'Come with me!' The witness, thinking the entity was Christ himself, answered: 'Dear Jesus, I don't want to go anywhere!' Several seconds later the being slowly rose up in the air and turbulence hit the witness. The humanoid disappeared just a dozen feet above the ground and the strange glow just went out. Mr. Jacek informed me that during the encounter he became cold and began to sweat."

Around 10 years after this incident something very similar was witnessed by Mr. Marek. On May 16th 2009 along he and his friend lit a campfire on a hill in close to his farm to cook some sausages (this is a traditional method of outdoor cooking). The men were surprised by a sudden spring downpour of rain. Quickly trying to seek cover, Mr. Marek hid in the in the woods near the farm in order to wait for the rain to abate. The other man was close by but could not see the following events.

The witness related to Arek Miazga that the whole sighting lasted only a matter of seconds. While sheltering from the rain he could hear some scratching sounds as if something was sliding down the roof. When he looked in the direction of the sounds, he could see a dark entity standing just in the corner of the barn.

"The being clearly stared at him for a second or two but then disappeared behind a nearby building. Slightly concerned, he rushed to inspect but found nothing. He stated that the figure was about 6 ft tall and was of very dark, nearly black color (but with a lighter face). According to Mr. Marek, it had arm-length black hair and a cloak similar to priest's gown" – the researcher said.

He added that unexplained things in Glinik seemed to concentrate in several locations. But the local residents were not happy with the paranormal notoriety that their village had gained and their tendency for sharing these uncanny experiences was officially condemned by the local parish priest. Those who have encountered these events prefer to stay in the background and feel insulted by the critics who claim: "That such things simply could not happen in our village."

In 2013 Arek received many offers from both TV and newspaper journalists all of whom were looking for sensational stories from the Glinik area. He refused them all saying that he would not break the confidence of witnesses but the media buzz caused many potential witnesses to remain quiet thus making further research much more difficult.

"The Glinik case is both bizarre and unique so it is not a surprise that it thrilled so many journalists. But today I do not talk with them anymore because on too many occasions they have simply distorted what I have had to say in an attempt to sensationalise these events. Regardless of the media our comprehension of things that are happening in that village is very limited and Glinik shows us one of the many UFO phenomenon's' faces that extend far beyond the limits of the extraterrestrial hypothesis" – Arek summarised.

Quotation sources

Arek Miazga Archives / arekmiazga.blogspot.com

Chapter 20

THE CZĘSTOCHOWA UFO ZONE

UFO chasing Grzegorz • Osson's Hill encounters • UFO over medieval castle
Falcon Hills UFO Zone • Flap of high strangeness

CZĘSTOCHOWA is the spiritual capital of Poland. The Jasna Góra Monastery (lit. Luminous Mount) holds the most venerated icon of the Black Madonna – allegedly painted by St. Luke. The Black Madonna is known all over the world and even incorporated in to Voodoo as Erzulie Dantor (due to the Polish soldiers of Napoleon who had brought the Marian cult into Santo Domingo in the early 19th century). There is also a centuries-long custom of walking pilgrimages to Jasna Góra held mostly before the local holiday on August 15th. The longest distance is around 320 miles of walking to pay homage to the miraculous icon while one of the most populous is the pilgrimage of the Rzeszów area – deemed the most religious region of the country.

It can not be excluded that many Glinik inhabitants also participated in the annual pilgrimage to Częstochowa which also coincidentally holds it own anomalous zone. In fact it is comprised of two areas one located in the south-eastern part of the city, in the Osson's Hill area and the second a further 6 miles to the south-east, in vicinity the of Sokole Góry (Falcon's Hill) in the Olsztyn Commune.

Częstochowa (with a population figure similar to Orlando, FL in the USA or Nottingham in the UK) is also northern top of the so called Jura region with picturesque limestone rocks and numerous ruins of medieval castles and strongholds. In this part of the city, near the local foundry (once one of the biggest steel-producing factories in Europe) there is a large rocky hill. At first glance it is no different from other hills in the region but upon close inspection one can see that

Osson's Hill is in fact a large bunker. The structure is a vast concrete, underground (now empty) basin once used as a water container for steel production purposes. This huge structure coming out of the rock, scrubs and sands makes the hill looks somewhat post-apocalyptic. This strange impression is deepened by the Holy Virgin statue built in the middle of the biggest rock. According to opinions of some researchers this location is also a theater for some very mysterious aerial phenomena. Local residents began to share their experiences when Grzegorz Tarczyński's story first emerged. This middle-aged, friendly man lives in the center of Częstochowa, in the summer of 2002 along with three other people experienced things so strange that he decided to share it openly, asking the local community: "Have you also seen this?" "Yes, we have!" – replied some in a somewhat perplexed voice.

Grzegorz Tarczyński UFO contact

Osson's Hill obtained its name from a man who once ran the local glider school. It is located in the uninhabited city perimeters but close to a number of quite busy roads that thousands of people pass by everyday on their way to work and school. Predziszów – one of the neighboring hills derives its name from an ancient-Polish word for *bizarre* what suggest that the early inhabitants might have witnessed something strange in the region also.

But the area became famous thanks to much a recent incident. It was in the late summer of 2002 when Grzegorz Tarczyński received a telephone call from his brother working at a gas distribution center at the foot of Osson's Hill.

"Come and take a look" – he said.

Grzegorz remembers that it was a Sunday, quite late at night. He then left his friends company and drove home to collect his binoculars. His father decided to join him as he had some time on his hands. They did not expect that it would turn into a very close, life-changing encounter with an intelligent object.

"When we found ourselves at that location, my brother told me that along with his work colleague they had observed something truly extraordinary over some nearby fields" – Grzegorz started his story.

"Soon it appeared again and danced over the area, going up and down and changing colors. With binoculars I could see that the object was composed of some sort of energy. At one point the object became red and ejected a streak of bluish smoke. After about half-a-hour of constant maneuvering, a point of light jumped off the main object. I could see it circling the big ball that brought forth some kind of electric discharge. Then both objects merged into

one. *The object now finally convinced me that it could not be some form of ball lightning or some sort of flying toy.*"

Time passed and the small object was still visible in the distance. Grzegorz said that despite the mysterious atmosphere and growing curiosity, they decided to return home. It was about midnight when he shook hands with his brother and soon drove off. But just a few hundred yards away he suddenly hit the brakes.

"At that moment I realised that it could be the last chance in my life to see the UFO at a close distance. Some may take my actions as being somewhat cinematic or dramatic but this is how it really happened. I turned my car down a dusty road, drove a while and put the hazard warning lights on. It seemed that the object reacted and after a while it became clear that it was coming in our direction. It stopped very close to us and issued a sequence of lights identical in frequency to the hazard lights of our Daewoo Matiz car. It was low over the ground. We were astounded but on the other hand it was also quite traumatic. I slowly drove back and rushed towards the city. The UFO followed us but then we lost it from sight" – he added.

This bizarre experience absorbed Grzegorz's thoughts for many days afterwards. Working close to the area of the hill, he tried to ask some other local people about reports of unidentified lights but with no result. After a while some friends of his informed him of a number of people who may also have witnessed the sighting but the information was second hand and of little relevance. What's more is that just after being chased by the luminous sphere, Grzegorz called the Police but the officer-on-duty explained to him that "they cannot respond" in any way whatsoever. He also tried to contact various media outlets but all to no avail.

As time went by Grzegorz Tarczyński admitted that the summer night's encounter of 2002 had changed his life forever. After meticulous a data gathering effort and numerous visits to the area, he has compiled quite an archive of UFO encounters in what he called the Częstochowa anomalous zone.

UFOs in the zone

Before I made contact with Grzegorz Tarczyński in 2005, I also received several other reports of unexplained events. The most intriguing took place in the 1950s in the Srocko village located not far away from Osson Hill. On an evening trip to the water well, a local woman noticed a light approaching her from the direction of the forest. At first she took it for her neighbor returning home with a lamp as he used to do and she even called him by name. But instead of answer, she could only hear a strange buzzing sound.

In no time at all she was confronted by a large sphere of light emitting a cracking noise. She immediately realised that it must be one of the objects she had heard of and without any hesitation she bolted, spilling all the water from her buckets. The woman who was very dependable and down-to-earth was in fact my great-grandmother (the author).

Grzegorz Tarczyński also came across several reports of early activity in the Osson Hill area. For example in 1988 a man saw pillars of light hovering in the air, which were performing bizarre maneuvers. A characteristic element of the Częstochowa UFO sightings involving a smaller object circling the main one appeared also in a sighting from the Stradom district, located a few miles away from the hill, where according to Rzepecki a mother and two teenage sons observed a *hazy*, disc-shaped object encircled by some sort of dot:

"The object was hovering over a tree located just 55 yards away. […] It was white, very thin and seemed to be made of fog in the witnesses' opinion but with clearly visible contours. In its central part there was a kind of protuberance. Moreover, it was encircled by a small point of light, also white in color, making one round per second in clockwise a direction. […] Then the object changed position and moved over their neighbor's house. It was about 45 ft in diameter."

There were also other sightings from the same time period when Grzegorz and his father encountered the intelligent sphere. Some years later he received a letter from a man living in the Raków district. Late at night in August of 2002 the man observed from the window of his flat an object with twinkling colorful lights.

"The object was disc-shaped. It then darted away, stopped and then circled over the foundry grounds" – he wrote.

"Then it appeared over the speedway stadium and the train station. I know that it was UFO. No conventional craft would be able to make these kind of maneuvers. Next it suddenly came to a standstill very close to our location, just over the school. It all happened so quickly that I was astounded. I stood in the window wondering what on earth it could be but after a while I came to realise that I was also under observation!"

In 2011 two other reports emerged. The first was from April 20th where a group of people visiting a limestone quarry in vicinity of Osson's Hill, observed an orange object ejecting a small sphere very high up in the sky. Then both UFOs took off in unison and began to reappear alternately one after another.

"At about 10:10 pm I saw from my kitchen window a flash of orange light" – reported a witness to the events from December 2011.

"I took my binoculars and saw two luminous points encircling one another.

At some point one stopped and the second one began to head in my direction, then it came to a standstill for about 4-5 minutes before darting off towards Osson's Hill. I could see two other points or objects in its center."

Other sightings involve mysterious flashes of light over the mountain (resembling lightning) or small, white and unbelievably quick objects that appear in that area even during the daytime. There are even several photos and videos of alleged unidentified objects over the hill. Most can be explained as *blurfos* but there is one especially interesting video. Grzegorz Tarczyński took the video during one of his first visits there with his then new digital camera. On the daytime movie (in MOV format) one can see a flying dark sphere that at one point splits in two and continue on its flight.

In a short time Osson's Hill became a mecca for teenage adventurers and amateur paranormal researchers. Searching for possible answers I have hypothesised that the super-heavy construction can in some way generate geological tensions that could appear as alleged earth-lights.

This theory is not able to explain apparently intelligently controlled objects that some witnesses have reported but it may well explain the unidentified lights. Moreover, the UFO zone in Częstochowa is not constrained to the Osson's area but covers a broader territory. Its next location which is also known for its higher amount of UFO activity is located between the picturesque hills and rocks of Jura.

Falcons' Hills zone

Just six miles to the south-east from Osson's Hill, amongst white rocky hills and dense forests lay Olsztyn – a small town located at the foot of the monumental Castle Hill. The 14th century Polish King, Casimir the Great rebuilt the local rock fortress into a vast stronghold. The ruined complex of Olsztyn castle with its stony towers and 100 ft tall donjon (looking like a cigarette turned upside) has survived to our times and in now a popular tourist attraction.

This entire region is permeated with history and legends. One of the most recent ones was born in 1996 when people living in the castle area observed a mysterious spherical object that illuminated the eastern slope of the Castle Hill. To Mrs. Krystyna who woke up at 3:45 am in a room filled with light, it seemed dazzling. Trying to localise its source, she noticed a bright object on the rocks beneath the castle. Moments later it flew off but an intense glow appeared on other side of the hill. Shocked, she ran to awake her son.

According to the witnesses, the object changed positions and soon two other lights came on – one amongst the rocks and the second in the vicinity of the tower.

The latter moved up and down and in the opinion of the other witness, Mrs. N., its surface was covered with some kind of *'scales'* or *'bands'*. In the final phase of the sighting all of the UFOs changed positions and slowly began to move away. The smallest one (which moved up and down) flew in the direction of Przymiłowice.

In the late summer of 2004 Olsztyn village became a center of unusual UFO activity with several high strangeness incidents. One of the first encounters took place in the forests of the Falcon Hills bordering Przymiłowice from the south. At about 6 pm. two young friends went for a stroll. Walking along a dusty lane between the fields they noticed an outburst of a very bright light in a rectangular shape. It looked like a *screen with rounded edges the same color of burning magnesium* (very iridescent). It shot on and off after being viewed for just several seconds. The object disappeared over the old forest close to Falcon Hills from the north. Suddenly, the object reappeared in a flash, at first against the setting sun but then down into the treetops. This sequence was repeated and it seemed that the object landed somewhere in the woods just 300 yards away. Shocked and confused, the witnesses did not move from their location until dusk but the object did not reappear.

> *"From today's perspective it might seem that our behavior on that night was a bit silly. We had a once-in-lifetime possibility to approach a real mystery head on but instead we preferred to wait in the lane like a pair of assholes..."* – said one of the witnesses.

> *"Maybe it was the fact that the object looked unnatural that prompted us to stay in what we thought was a safe place. Small pine trees in the field to the west protected us from the site where the object would have landed. But when we were walking back, in a small clearing between the trees we could see a ruby-colored light (as if a type of laser) low over the ground. On the next day I searched all the forest. I could find no trace of anything unusual."*

It is worth to noting that the witnesses were deemed to be highly reliable and the location of the sighting lay in the territory where the mysterious light phenomenon called Świetlik haunted the local people for many decades (I discussed this in the first chapter).

Roughly around the same time, Mr. Andrzej T. – one of the last real farmers in the area, was on his way to pasture located amongst the hills south of the Falcons' Mountains. Passing slowly along the bank of the low forest, he noticed a *light* circling a woodless rocky hill surrounded by fields known as the Bald Mountain just half a mile away. The object was celadon-bright and oblong but of a rather angular shape.

"It was not too big" – he said.

"It just circled the hill and flew away. I though to myself: What the hell is that thing but I had to bring my cows back from the pasture. The hills behind village are desolate and this strange phenomenon gave me chills. However, to my great surprise, when I arrived at the pasture, I saw that object again flying from the other direction. It seemed that it was circling the area or doing some kind of survey."

Mr. Andrzej is a simple, hard-working, single man living with his elderly mother. He had seen many things in his life but the UFO really gave him the chills. Interestingly, for him this incident started a days-long sequence of strange experiences.

"Just a day after the initial UFO sighting, during my nighttime duties on the farm I noticed a strong light in front of the gate. It was just as if a car stood there with its headlights on. I approached it but it took off. Then I saw another light, as flat as a sheet of paper, taking off from the field on opposite side of the road. The next morning I had planned to go to the market in nearby Mstów. I woke up before sunset and went to tend my animals. Suddenly, I saw a round configuration of lights positioned high up in the sky but clearly visible. It was as if some kind of round-shaped object hovered just above me. Although it quickly flew off I was scared and decided to stay at home. This was the last time I witnessed any strange things in the area."

Then Mr. Andrzej learned from his neighbors that they saw strange lights too. Those objects weren't too spectacular but clearly anomalous in nature. It's also interesting that they appeared in a short period of several days and then disappeared for good. From that time nothing unusual has been seen in the area.

The 2004 flap of UFO sightings additionally involved two encounters with unidentified humanoid beings. The witness to the first of these, Mr. Marcin, was returning from an evening stroll with his dog and he decided to take a shortcut through the forest. All of a sudden a short person appeared at his side and as he related, it began to move around him in a *dancing* or *hopping* manner. It was dark at the time so he could only make out that the entity seemed small and skinny. Scared to death, he bolted home which fortunately was just a few hundred yards away. I would like to add that the location of all of these events can be enclosed on a map in a triangle with the side lengths of less than a mile each. The last incident took place just a mile to the east from this area, in a small clearing just over the village where three teenagers decided to light a bonfire. When bonfire's the flames had illuminated their surroundings, to their utter terror they noticed that a white face was looking at them from behind a small tree stump.

Kamil B. – today an entrepreneur – said that he was the first to see it. It seemed to him that the being must be either very small or was standing on all fours.

"It was intensely white in color, with a half-opened mouth. Its skin was wrinkle free but seemed stretched in some manner. In all it looked like a plaster cast" – he said. *"Its head was as that of human but stranger. The eyes were of a normal size but more round, black inside and probably with no eyelids."*

The other witness, Sławek K., related the same story. The boys had enough time to look at the head that was constantly hiding behind the tree stump. Panicked, they tried to insult it verbally in an attempt to make it go away (at first they took it for a prankster) and even threw sticks and stones in its direction. The head did not react to any of this. Possessing no cell-phones they could not call for assistance. They decided to go back the village but at first they had to extinguish the fire. At the same time as they were putting the fire out the face disappeared. Sick with terror and thinking that it would attack them in the grove of trees that separated them from the village; the boys trampled the last smoldering embers of the fire and ran home. Fortunately the white-faced intruder did not reappear.

They had no explanation for this sighing and neither do I (the author). Because this incident took place during the same period of time as the other sightings in Przymiłowice, it has led me to catalogue them into one large ufological event of high-strangeness. Both Sławek and Kamil pondered the possibility of any conventional explanations for their experience and said that the only idea that they came up with was that *the Face* could have be some kind gothic or metal weirdo wandering the forest at night in full make-up. But in hindsight the face looked too peculiar to be human.

The Przymiłowice UFO flap provided researchers with a good opportunity to study UFO-related psychology. The witnesses did not lie and showed absolutely no tendencies for hoaxing. They were normal members of the local community who experienced something out-of-ordinary but it was also proved uncomfortable for them to discuss or even publicise their stories.

For local people privacy and personal freedom is the highest priority. I know this fact well. I have lived here all of my life and know the witnesses personally. Surely you would like to know if I also saw a UFO in flap of 2004? I will of course not tell you as it is a private matter.

QUOTATION SOURCES

Piotr Cielebiaś and Michał Kuśnierz Archives / *infra.org.pl*

Chapter 21

THE RZESZÓW UFO ZONE

Photographic & video cases • UFO-probe over apartment house
Barrel-shaped UFO on video • New Year anomaly • Peripheral mysteries

THERE is a good case for Rzeszów to be called *the UFO capital of Poland*. For unknown reasons the city with around 185 thousands of it inhabitants is subjected to continued UFO activity, concentrating in the districts of New Town (Nowe Miasto), Słocina and Baranówka.

"UFO sightings come from post 1980s period where some resulted in photographic evidence" – says Arek Miazga who listed dozens of cases from that area. "Rzeszów's inhabitants reported both classic saucers and highly unusual objects. Remarkably, this unexplained activity is not restricted to the city's outskirts but also took place over densely populated housing complexes."

One example of such an incident involved 18-year-old Grzegorz who lived on the second floor of an apartment house in the Baranówka district. Late one night in August 1996 he was listening to a radio broadcast when a peculiar rumbling noise caught his attention. Looking outside the young man noticed *a black mass* flying at a distance of just 160 yards away and was just 200 feet above the ground. It looked like a typical flying saucer topped by a cupola and a tail end that resembled a *spoiler*.

Arek's archive is teeming with other cases proving that UFOs are lurking between apartment houses and above suburban areas both day and night. At times the elusive intelligence controlling those objects dropped its guard and allowed the fortunate witnesses to capture them on film.

Rzeszów UFO photos & videos

"It was in the year 2000, just before Christmas" – an anonymous female witness from Baranówka recounts. "I do not remember the exact hour but it was probably

A photograph from Baranówka (district of Rzeszów) from the year 2000. The anonymous female witness allegedly observed a number of strange lights maneuvering in front of the window and decided to snap a photo. She caught the object in flight over the apartment block (seen as a light in left upper side). Credit: Arek Miazga's Archive

between 6pm and 8pm. My attention was grabbed by a light outside. By the same window (located on 4th floor) I used to see airplanes descending in order to land at Jasionka airport.

But in this instance the object was too low and did not display the characteristic red, pulsating lights like the airplanes normally do. After a while it reappeared behind the building across from ours. 'Maybe some Technical University students are practicing with flying model?' – I thought but soon the object zigzagged in the air making a figure eight-shaped maneuver and moved from left to right.

Intrigued, I took my Minolta camera but the light was moving too fast for me to take a good photo. Then another object appeared to the left. It flew at a constant speed without any complicated maneuvers."

The woman managed to snap two motion blur photos of the object hovering over the apartment block opposite her. As she explained, the second object soon approached the zigzagging one and the two flew away together. According to her estimates both were more than 5 feet in diameter (they were roughly of the same width as window frames). The woman, who contacted Arek Miazga nine years

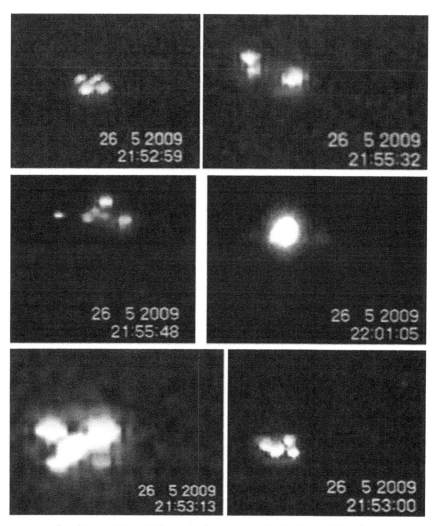

An alleged shape-shifting UFO over the Rzeszów area (Słocina-Tyczyn) filmed in 2009. (Credit: Arek Miazga's Archive)

after the sighting, claimed that she attempted to ask tenants in the neighboring house if they had seen anything extraordinary but was not sure what their reaction might be. Skeptics would say that the Baranówka inhabitant snapped a photo of a brilliant Moon peering from behind the apartment block but that possibility is easy to dismiss because the moon was not positioned in that part of the sky.

Another possible UFO of small dimensions was photographed on May 6th 2007 by a man who from his friend's house noticed an object over fields in direction of Biała. He grabbed the camera and took a more than minute-long video of the alleged UFO maneuvering near to a transmission tower. Applying the cameras zoom facility on lead to the lowering the picture quality but the UFO is still clear and the object's behavior cannot simply be explained in conventional terms.

On the night of May 26th 2009 a Rzeszów witness noticed from his balcony a number of unexplained lights twinkling above the suburban villages of Chmielnik and Tyczyn. With binoculars he could see that *the phenomenon* composed of several whirling lights so he decided to record it on video.

> *"In the first part of the video one can see the whirling, red-orange lights forming a shape resembling the number five on a dice. At about 9:55 pm only two objects (a red one and a fiery looking one) are rotating to the left at a high speed while the remaining light stood still. The entire aerial spectacle was very impressive. What's more is that another white ball of light soon joined the group of lights and then began to disappear and reappear alternately (both behind and in front of the light formation)"* – Arek says.

His archive of UFOs recorded over Rzeszów contains 10 more videos amongst which is also a video of a barrel-shaped rotating object shot on July 25th 2000 from New Town. Videotaping a unique cloud cover over the district, a local resident noticed an unidentified, dark oblong object entering his camera's viewfinder. It was heading west, flying awkwardly, i.e. with its side, (its longest part) to the fore. A bright white light could be seen on the upper sector of the object while in the final part of the video a streak of yellow light is seen emanating from its underside.

Older cases proved interesting also. At the turn of 31st December 1997 and New Year 1998 many people in the Rzeszów area observed a spherical orange object. At about 11:30 pm Jan Skroban and Maciej Robert, who were staying on St. Rocco's Hill waiting for a firework display that they had intended to videotape, noticed a brilliant orange sphere positioned high over the city.

> *"It came into view for about 10 seconds and then simply turned off. Despite their quick reaction they were not able to catch it on video. However at about 11:50 pm the object reappeared and the witnesses videotaped it with their VHS camera. It could be clearly seen that it was different from the fireworks exploding at a lower altitude"* – Arek explains. *"After about 40 seconds it disappeared. The next video of luminous ball was taken at 0:20 are. The object was pulsating with an intense orange light but just seconds later it went out. Then the same or very similar pulsating object appeared over the Słocina forests."*

Local press offices, startled by the numerous letters and reports, tried their best to explain away this mass New Year UFO sighting. Soon an explanation emerged that the whole event was caused by a military flare release. Journalists were allegedly contacted by a man from Krasny (nearly 2 miles to east from Rzeszów) who claimed to release a single flare at 11:50 pm but it could not explain its presence in other locations over a period of half an hour. Moreover, Dr Roman Ampel – an astrophysicist from Rzeszów, excluded any astronomical origin for the unidentified object.

Anomalies in suburbia

In recent times Rzeszów city limits and suburbia have also witnessed spectacular UFO incidents with two interesting examples from May 10th 2012. At about 3 pm workers at a warehouse observed a movement in the cloudless sky. As it turned out, it was a group of spherical objects coming from various directions to a point where a *screw-shaped* mother craft was stationed.

"They all stopped by an object that after watching it for quite a while I would compare nits shape to that of a screw-thread. The speed and characteristics of the flight of the small objects was unlike any of the airplanes heading to Jasionka airport. Two spheres flew away after some maneuvers in the air. The screw-shaped one and the rest just disappeared."

The second encounter of much more direct character manner took place in Hermanowa. At about 9:30 pm a local man, describing himself as a *rationalist*, went outside to put his car in the garage and was startled by the sight of approaching light…

"It soon stopped about 85-100 feet away from me, just above my neighbor's house. It was only 6-10 feet above the roof of his house. Then I saw an identical object following the same flight path which was also in total silence. It too soon stopped over the house exactly the same as the first ball of light. After about 20 seconds it veered off at an angle of 130 degrees and flew away and soon the other light followed it" – said the witness adding that both objects were just about a foot in diameter.

On June 6th 2011, at about 8 pm Mrs. Beata who went outside with her dog saw a *heavy flying artifact* passing over a part of Baranówka which was adjacent to open fields and trees.

"I remember being followed by a girl with German shepherd dog. My dog off course felt its presence and pulled the leash back. The sun was setting and then to my great surprise I saw something crossing the sky over one of the

houses. The object was elliptic and was seemingly made of some heavy metal. Something on its surface twinkled quite brightly. Although the dog was pulling me back, I watched the object in awe. I decided to wait for the girl to catch up to me but when she was just a few steps from me, UFO went behind the trees" – Mrs. Beata said.

"The sight instantly absorbed my mind. The object was flying just above the treetops, 55-75 yards away. I don't know what I have seen. Maybe I was delusional? – I thought but my mind rejected any such notion: It was so close to me!

The object was oval, about 30-50 feet long, and 15-30 feet across. Its color resembled dull metal. It was completely soundless but emitted some bright outbursts of light (as if some lights were positioned along its perimeter)" – she added.

Interviewing the woman Arek became sure that she reported to him an accurate account triggered by some unexplained, uncontrollable phenomenon. But how could it be that that such a massive object was seen by just one witness? Such a situation stands in contrary to logic and today's reality where it is very hard to conceal anything, especially in the city.

Mrs. Beata saw the object on Sunday, in close vicinity to a large housing estate. She is sure that the experience was real but on the other hand, independent corroboration is missing. So either other witnesses preferred to stay silent or the phenomenon itself is controlling the course of the confrontation with *human intelligence.*

The same principle manifested itself in a sighting from another peripheral part of Rzeszów that in time of writing the book was still an ongoing case. A mother and daughter from Słocina – a district of detached houses in the eastern part of the city witnessed several UFO encounters with the initial one mimicking the features of Mrs. Beata's experience.

"With my daughter I observed an object flying low over the ground that resembled a plate turned upside down. A silvery-metallic thing was flying soundlessly through the air and then made a sharp turn and disappeared. The sighting lasted about 2 minutes. What's more is that the object possessed a row of small windows on its bottom edge" – said Mrs. Anna (63) – a teacher who on September 23rd observed the flying saucer.

Arek established that this UFO seen over the garden plots was about 25 feet in diameter. After several months he was contacted by the women again, learning that they had witnessed another strange manifestation this time in close vicinity to their house. One of the witnesses even tried to approach it, smelling a strong odor that it apparently gave off.

> "The sighting occurred at about 5:30 on March 5th 2013. The daughter of Mrs. Anna opened the door to let her cat go out but the animal momentarily hesitated and it literally went crazy. She looked up and saw unexplained lights against the dark sky a quarter of mile away. At first she took it for an airplane but they were stationary" – Arek explains.

> "With binoculars the woman noticed that they were strapped to a dark-metallic cupola with a flat bottom and lights positioned on the lower part (so it was quite similar to that seen on September 23rd). It was hovering about 650 feet over some houses in the area. Soon the object flew away eastwards. When the woman approached the area above where the object had been seen, her nostrils were hit by an unidentified, sweet and suffocating smell."

Despite Arek's press calls, no other witnesses emerged. The Słocina women who have stayed anonymous remain in contact with the researcher and keep cameras ready just in case of the UFO reappears. But their example is not exceptional. For all those years many other people reported experiences based on the same scenario and Arek is well aware that tracking the phenomenon in practice would be a permanent cat and mouse display. Therefore he is instead seeking clues in Keel and Vallée books repeating their most notable conclusion that UFOs are real although they are not what they seem to be.

QUOTATION SOURCES

Arek Miazga's Archive / arekmiazga.blogspot.com

Miazga A., *UFO nad Podkarpaciem*, v. 1, Ropczyce 2013 (ebook).

Chapter 22

FLYING HUMANOIDS

*Man with arms crossed • Angel or alien? • Long-haired humanoid
Manasterz humanoid • Lelów animal-like being & Niemojków robotic owl*

IN 2008 I received a call from Mrs. Izydora K. – a 71-year-old woman from Szczecinek (zachodniopomorskie) who had reported an encounter with unexplained phenomenon but did not know where to seek advice. She reported that in March that year a long with her husband they went on a weekend car trip to the Borne Sulinowo forests which are dotted with the ruins of post-Soviet military complexes. In the early afternoon they parked their car by one of the old buildings and took a short stroll. Mrs. Izydora's husband soon left her for a while to take a look at one of the former Soviet buildings. She did not like being left on her own so she chose to wait for her husband and went to stand close to their parked car.

Spring was in the air but it had not yet arrived. All at once the witness saw a misty shape appear just several steps from her in front of some trees. The closer she looked the more it resembled a large human figure with its arms crossed. Mrs. Izydora's analytic and still very sharp mind instantly recognised that the situation was far from normal so she quickly tried to back away.

"It was just the outline of a male silhouette flying several feet over the ground" – she said. "The interior of this phantom seemed hazy as if camouflaged. I stood petrified with fear, temporarily unable to move but somehow I managed to get to the car. At the same time the being began flying in my direction."

Due to fear and anxiety or the humanoids strange influence, the elderly lady felt weak at the knees but remained fully conscious. In seconds the transparent *thing* passed over her and disappeared between the treetops. Fearing that her husband would also came across *the phantom*, Mrs. Izydora was happy to see him returning. She immediately ordered him to go home excusing herself saying she felt unwell. After two days of being in two minds she finally decided to reveal the story to her family members. Though relieved at telling them it brought no definite explanations for what she had encountered.

Most witnesses of these alleged flying humanoids encounters have problems in trying to classify their experiences because they are in their own anomalous category. I have heard comparisons to encounters with angel's devils from old folk tales. In some of the flying humanoids encounters they can perhaps be described as brushes with living folklore. For example, if Marian B.'s experience had taken place several decades earlier, it would be easily taken for angelical or Holy Virgin apparition. But in the space race era the witness and his companions, brought up in an atheist, socialist country knew that is impossible to met holy beings although the possibility of encountering a space citizen could not be excluded.

> "It was in the late autumn of 1969. We were coming back from cinema in Pieńsk town located in Lower Silesia region" – Mr. Marian said.

> "We took a shortcut near the fields and chatted all the way. Suddenly, when I looked at a young oak tree 10-15 feet away, I saw that strange figure. Initially, I was shocked, so were my friends. It stood there and watched us in a strange way. I must admit that my hair momentarily stood on end. In height it was nearly equal to us. The being's face was gray and featureless but had clearly visible neck and head surrounded by a delicate yellow glow. The lower parts of its body were emanating a bluish light. Although they were brilliantly illuminated they cast no light on their surroundings."

Despite the being's face being just a gray mass, Mr. Marian and his colleagues could feel its gaze. At first glance the bright halo around its head would suggest its angelic origin but the witness was sure that it was instead something or someone not from heaven but from outer space. This encounter witnessed by four young men did not end with the being simply disappearing in plain sight, at least not direct. Instead the young men chose the option. Instead of trying to escape they tried to catch the being.

The humanoid's reaction was instantaneous – it backed away and began to float away, moving just inches over the ground and maneuvering over trees and scrubland so it must have made of solid matter – Mr. Marian noticed. They chased the being toward a railway embankment where it accelerated and turned into a hollow leading to the other side of the embankment where it disappeared.

The witness recounts that the entire area was drowned in darkness but the glowing oddity was nowhere to be seen. This mind-boggling experience was engraved in witness's minds forever. Of the three participants that are still alive only Mr. Marian B. decided to reveal his story publicly gaining more than 100,000 views on YouTube.

Another high-strangeness report came from a doctor who is now holding an important position in the administrational office of the public health service. The incident too place in the autumn of 2000 between Koniewo village and the historical city of Lidzbark Warmiński (north-western Poland). On that night the witness and his friend were on their way home to the city after visiting a fellow video gamer.

> "Half-way between the city and Koniewo there is a small valley with two sharp curves in the road surrounded by trees" – he informed researcher Michał Kuśnierz.

> "I was returning with my friend on our bicycles. I could even remember that we talked about a private gym used by our colleague. We then rode along the straight section of road leading to the valley.

> It was dark and cold but the moonlight was so intense that we could clearly see the surroundings. After peddling along for a short while something urged both of us to look right. Against the trees we clearly could see a flying entity. It was flying in horizontal position with its face looking right at us."

Without much talking, the witnesses fled from the scene as fast as they could. The entity that had crossed their path and disappeared amongst the trees looked to be very large, was male and had long hair. This terrifying experience, according to my informers account, was accompanied by some loud banging noises. The witnesses soon reached a friends house in Koniewo and asked his mother to drive them back to Lidzbark. They feared that the grayish oddity would wait for them on the road and they were scared to go back on unaccompanied.

Situations like those above are hard to comment on. You may not believe in them until you meet with the witnesses yourself. For the readers of this book high-strangeness stories may sound like another cheap tabloid story and for that reason some UFO researchers from all over the world tend to sometimes stay away from them and not put their names and reputation in jeopardy. But *de facto* these incidents remain as the missing link between ufology, the paranormal and folklore. The first years of the 21st century brought a flap of flying humanoid encounters in Mexico with several successful attempts to immortalise the phenomenon on videos and photos. At the same time similar incidents occurred in Poland although it did not result in any video or photos of these strange flying humanoids.

The first incident took place in fields around Lelów – a small rural town known for its Jewish-related history and being the location of the tomb of the world-famous tzadik of Lelow Rabins, David Biderman. On September 24th 2004 local people observed a number of people in orange overalls crossing the pastures but took them for surveyors or land improvement workers of some kind. Then at about 10 am an elderly farmer, Józef Niepsuj, noticed one of these beings in his field. Trying to approach it, the orange humanoid figure (definitely not a bird in his opinion) rose up and flew away.

It is possible that the encounter was witnessed by more than 30 people in total. Some added that the figure's attire resembled an overall with dark bands along the back. Others added that it changed colors while flying away. This intriguing case remains unexplained and many of the witnesses (mostly elderly local farmers) were reluctant to share their accounts.

In 2014 Arek Miazga was contacted by Mrs. Anna from Manasterz located 18 miles south of Rzeszów (in the Glinik area) who in 2005 along with her family observed a tall, dark flying figure slowly descending into woods just a few hundred yards away. Some of her family members rushed to the woods to try and find the mysterious visitor.

> *"I live in close vicinity to the forest. On that day we noticed a human-looking figure in the air (with discernable head and limbs) that was flying or rather sliding down"* – she reported to Arek Miazga.

> *"It had neither parachute nor any other things visible. Moreover, it was slowly moving around its axis. My relatives estimated that it was only 30 feet over the treetops. When they reached the woods where it had supposedly landed, they found nothing but they could feel some king of pressure in the air and a strange atmosphere surrounded the area."*

But possibly the most outrageous meeting with a flying humanoid took place in August 1991 in the Mojków area. Up until this point all the previous mentioned flying oddities seemed to be living, breathing, human-like entities but in this case the witness (in circumstances similar to that of Lelów) encountered a thing he described as *robotic* or *automatic*.

Early in the morning a local farmer was leading his cow to a pasture and saw an object that gleamed in the sunshine just 165 yards away. He approached it with curiosity and was startled to see a four foot tall bowling-shaped thing covered with metallic scales. Two glassy eyes nearly 4 inches wide and a small tube in front made the object resemble a large *mechanic owl* constantly turning from left to right.

The farmer pressed by other duties, had to go leave this spectacle but other witnesses said that about 7am the object rose up in the air and flew in the direction of the nearby Myszkowice village.

Such cases in my opinion cannot be explained in any conventional way and those with more-than-one witness gains additional credibility. Questions on the nature and origin of the flying humanoids phenomenon multiply and their mystery is deepening with each new case. But there is possibly a slight behavioral line connecting it with the overall UFO phenomenon. Manifestations of flying humanoids include the same anomalous features: evasiveness, lack of clear intentions and contact attempts. A celebrity-like nature of UFOs and some other paranormal phenomena is reflected in the fact that they like to show off, to be looked at and to evoke controversies. That is in fact the only specific aftermath of all similar phenomena. The same applies to the flying humanoids. If they were extraterrestrial scouts roaming the isolated places of out planet simply to scare the unsuspecting witnesses, they would be surely acting in an outstandingly reckless way.

QUOTATION SOURCES

Piotr Cielebiaś' and Michał Kuśnierz's Archives / infra.org.pl

B. Rzepecki, Bliskie spotkania z UFO w Polsce, Tarnów 1995.

Chapter 23

CONSCIOUSNESS-RELATED CASES

UFO on the highway • Sztum encounter • IQ test onboard UFO
Substitute memories • Animal processio

CONSCIOUSNESS-RELATED aspects of UFO encounters forms probably the most enigmatic and significant part of the phenomenon but also the most puzzling one. From witnesses' reports emerge an overall pattern indicating that unidentified objects can control witnesses at their will and are able to induce fear, confusion but on the other side, some close encounters are affecting the witness consciousness and sometimes even their intellectual grow. Another perplexing ability is to introduce the witnesses in an extended variation of reality where they see things invisible to others or sights that are simply impossible.

In the middle of the city

At 1 am on July 8th 2007 Mrs. Joanna – a businesswoman from Dąbrowa Górnicza (śląskie) was driving home on the highway to her home in Mydlice district. It must be highlighted here at the very beginning that the Silesian-Dabrovian urban area is a huge cluster of neighboring cities and towns inhabited by about 3 million people. It is the industrial center of Southern Poland teeming with life and littered with huge housing estates. Culturally and historically the region is divided into the Zagłebie and Silesian regions which more than 100 years ago was shared between Russia and Germany.

But let us return to her encounter. The woman in question claims that at one point while driving along the highway, she was assaulted by a strange bluish, indescribable object. Afraid, she called her business-partner on the phone informing him that she was observing a *UFO*. The man ignored her remarks saying

A painting made by the witness of the Dąbrowa Górnicza incident when after being chased by a strange object it then hovered over the woman's apartment block and sent down a number of strange "spheres". The woman is sure that the reality or her consciousness was altered by the strange force. (Credit: Mrs. Joanna / Infra.org.p Archive)

that she must be delusional or something similar. At the very same moment Mrs. Joanna noticed that the object was running parallel to her car and cast a bizarre marine-blue light over the area. She could also clearly see that it was ball-shaped but was composed of some king of bluish, plasmatic mass.

> *"I realised that this thing was chasing me"* – she said. *"Terrified, I changed the course I usually take to get home and went a different way. Suddenly I could not see the object in the air. But when I reached my apartment house, I saw it once again. It was still in the sky as if waiting for me. It seemed to me that the energy the phenomenon was composed of was 'intelligent'. Above the clouds there was a strange bluish object looking as if composed of some kind of energy but at the same time was also metallic. It was rotating clockwise. It was a fascinating sight. The object's size was immense"* – she said.

Mrs. Joannas' housing block above which the object was hovering was surrounded by numerous similar apartment houses. What is more, she went on to add that despite the late hour, the area was not deserted. She could remember seeing a man returning home. A grayish glow in a number of windows suggested that some people were watching still up and watching TV. But did anyone see this gigantic whirling object? The answer is *no*. I have not been able to locate any other witnesses from either the highway area or from other local residents.

This incident became even more controversial after what the object did next. Mrs. Joanna said that when she was taken aback and was more that a little afraid of getting too close to the object when the UFO burst into life with releasing a fabulous and picturesque exhibition.

> *"Those object looked like stars. At first they were ejected from the object and began to fall down towards the ground. It seemed to me that they were descending towards the houses but instead they fell on land that had no buildings on it. It was all soundless and did not resemble any kind of meteorites or fireworks. At this point I decided it was time to get away from there..."* – Mrs. Joanna wrote.

That night the witness slept at her friend's house who lived not too far away. Her friend confirmed that she was indeed very scared and frantically tried to close all the windows and shut the curtains in his apartment when she arrived. Mrs. Joanna is a very reliable and credible individual and she was very concerned (and even scared) for several weeks afterwards. She was also aware that to some her sighting may be quite unbelievable. The woman also added that the object she observed seemed to be made from something solid but added that the whole experience seemed to take place on some other plane of reality. In other words, an*other state of consciousness or perception* would the best way of describing her experience.

I could not find any clues to suggest that the witness had a history of hoaxing or that the plasmatic UFO was simply a mistaken identity of the city lights reflecting from the clouds surface. The woman had no history of delusion or hallucinations. On the other hand it is impossible to give any conventional answer to what she had experienced. It was in my opinion probably an extreme example of a type of UFO sighting that other people have also witnessed in many different parts of the world. This type of sighting includes situations where a spectacular unidentified object appears in highly populated areas and the manifestation public is only observed by one or two spectators.

For example, in 1990 Mrs. Edyta S. and her sister went for an evening stroll with their dog which began acting strangely and drew their attention to an object hovering over the apartment house. A huge, ring-shaped object emitting a pale haze and an audible hum that literally filled their ears. Mrs. Edyta remembered that she could see the dog moved its muzzle as if barking but only the humming sound from the object could be heard.

The last conscious memory of the sisters was the ring-shaped object approached them. She then remembered it zigzagging off in the distance. How something like this could happen in reality over a housing estate full of people with only two witnesses is extremely puzzling. Or maybe the encounters like this do not take place in an everyday plane of reality but rather in something completely different?

UFO IQ testing

Amongst many different sightings that I have featured in this book, there are many involving consciousness-related aftereffects. The remaining cases embrace these unique experiences which are very troublesome for researchers of the UFO phenomenon around the world and not just in Poland. One of the most unusual encounters that I come across took place in Sztum on September 20th 1979 and involved two men who were at the time doing some maintenance work on a property. Piechota and Rzepecki deemed this case as witnesses' intelligence test and this label should speak for itself.

> *"It all started when I leaned down to drink some water from the tap in the backyard. I drank a mouthful but the second sip could not pass through my mouth. I could feel a kind of tightness grasping my body and something metallic passed by the corner of my eye. I immediately thought that it was an airplane crash so I fell to the ground yelling at my companion to do the same"*
> – he said.

But no roar filled the air and the ground did not tremble. When the silence had fallen, Mr. Mirosław G. got up and saw the most bizarre thing in all of his life.

20 feet above him there was a huge, silvery object resembling two huge arrowheads connected by a cross-shaped section. The thing quickly transformed into a flattened sphere resembling a saucer.

The other witness, Mr. Krysztof K., at that time was inside of the summerhouse:

"I saw the brilliant sphere that was descending to the ground. I felt no fear just amazement. Seeing Mirek slowly getting up from the ground, I rushed in his direction and entered a kind of milky-pink haze. In just a second or two we found ourselves in-between glass-like walls. We could not see the bottom which was covered with a fog that felt like cotton wool. Although it was not pressing against me it acted like a kind of numbing agent. My leg shook and a high-pitching sound rang in my head" – he said.

Mirosław G. felt the pressure so strongly that at some point it disfigured his face but soon it was gone and the next, much more bizarre phase of the experience followed.

"Suddenly I saw some cuboids coming out of the mist. They seemed to be its creations – something among its mass. I tried to lean over them and realised they are solid so I sat in one. Then a strange feeling came over me, similar to being excited but at the same moment some words and phrases began to form in my mind, words and phrases that I did not use in my everyday life. They mainly concerned certain sciences and their flow was very fast and somewhat overwhelming. It seemed to me that a bunch of mixed and meaningless terms were crowding in into my mind" – he said.

For the next witness the experience resulted in a brush with the intelligence controlling the whole phenomenon. It all happened when the strange influence over him (numbness) abated and he regained consciousness and bodily control.

"I realised that it must be a kind of UFO experience. So I tried to communicate with the 'force', asking about its origins and its aims. But I heard nothing. 'What do you know about semi-conductors?' – I asked in my thoughts and that was the first time I heard a clear negative answer. Those thoughts did not come from me. I asked about semi-conductors because I am an electronic technician by profession. 'What can you tell me about the matter?' – I asked. 'It is penetrable' – I heard. But then the intelligence forced me to turn back and touch the manifestations in the mist. I saw a small screen with pictures of lakes, images from Sztum and other pictures. 'What is that?' – I was asked by them. For unknown reasons I told them: 'It's a city' though I recognised it as Sztum."

Their experience soon ended just abruptly as it had started. The mysterious matter vanished in a fraction of second and both of them fell to the ground. What is interesting is that in the days after the strange experience both of men went for psychiatric testing that showed no aberrations. In the opinion of an expert they were not delusional and the story was coherent. Krzysztof K. was also subjected to regressive hypnosis but it did not result in any details other than those he consciously remembered. He only admitted that he did not receive anything information from the encounter but was instead rather *drained of his own knowledge.*

Problematic encounters

On February 22nd 1982 in outskirts of Jasło a male witness was suddenly woken up in the middle of the night. Looking outside he could see a greenish light over a grove of trees some 330 yards away. The light came from a large object of the same color which was rhythmically pulsating with light and growing in size.

"Everything went deadly quiet" – Arek Miazga explains.

"What is interesting, he recounted to me that the ball of light seemed to be a living creature, not a technical, nuts-and-bolts object. But the process of observation was very unusual. He claimed that for reasons unknown, he could see it in normal way but also from the rear."

This split of vision was not the only original aspect of the encounter. The witness was sure that he was so mesmerised by the sight of the object that when the object had disappeared, he opened the terrace doors and intended to jump off the balcony to try and find the UFO!

"Although the green ball was gone, its glow could still be seen over the valley. At that point the witness heard in his head a kind of metallic voice saying: 'You cannot go there.' He returned to his room at 2:10 am. In his opinion, during the encounter he was in some kind of altered state of perception. The UFO itself was beautiful and had a kind of soothing influence on him" – Arek reported.

During the same period, although the witness is not now sure of the encounters exact date, two workers at the glass foundry in Piechowice experienced another very controversial encounter resulting in changes to their consciousness. It was about 1 pm when the witnesses' truck drove along the narrow highlands way to Szklarska Poręba. To the left of the driver there was the picturesque sight of Stony Pits

"It was just a reflection in the windshield, so nothing spectacular but I was forced to check what it was. So I stopped at the wayside, turned the engine off and got out of the truck. My colleague followed me" – Mr. Marek said.

"I was not very impressed with what we saw but my colleague knelt down

and made the sign of the cross which I found to be very weird. While we were standing there and watching this ball of light, a long line of cars had aligned behind us. It was amazing because we stood there for only a second. All the drivers were quietly sitting in their vehicles and no one seemed irritated or annoyed. The ball of light we saw momentarily shot off, heading in the Szlarska Poreba direction. It disappeared in a second. Although the whole sighting was only seconds long, I could felt as if time had been frozen..." – he added.

The object both men saw looked like a 60 foot across ball made of crystal glass but it was not transparent and reflected the suns rays. For them the whole sighting was just 30 seconds long but shortly after Mr. Marek realised that something was wrong with the whole scenario. On the next day he went to the exact location and realised that it was impossible for them to stand by the wayside. The place where his friend had knelt a day ago abruptly ended in a sharp drop so he would immediately have fallen over the edge. Also the traffic at that location was rather quiet and could not have gathered so many motorists in just a matter of seconds.

So what had they experienced in reality and why were their conscious memories substituted by a different version? And who implanted it into their minds? Mr. Marek's experience was so perplexing to him that merely thinking about it caused him a lot of distress. Added to this he also experienced long lasting sleeping problems.

A UFO encounter may cause a man to see things that did not take place in our plane of reality but they are objectively real. Unfortunately the fact that we cannot measure or reproduce such effects in the laboratory makes the study of such experiences by contemporary science virtually impossible. UFO intelligence (or what) is apparently treating people like animals, being able to manipulate them at will. If we speak about animals, it is also worth to noting a rather special case that I helped research in 2011.

In 2007 Mrs. Magda from Częstochowa was returning late at night from her boss' office. As a keen driver she was driving fast and was surprised to see a light approaching her at speed. Decelerating and thinking that it was a cyclist, she noticed that the object was instead a kind of brilliant spherical light hovering over the ground at the height of her car roof. The object seemed glued to Mrs. Magda's car and followed the terrified witness for several miles. Her report of the encounter with the UFO is interesting in itself but just before the object's disappearance a very unusual thing happened. "Magda hit the brakes upon seeing animals crossing the road in front of her. But it was not just a single deer or a hare" – Grzegorz said. "In her opinion it was a flock composed of different animals: deer, hares, boars etc. It looked as if someone had collected them together from the forest and then forced them to cross the road at certain locality. Surely this was not a natural occurrence?"

Grzegorz is right that such a situation could not happen in nature. Were the animals also brainwashed by and unknown type of interaction with the UFO? Or maybe the incident did not take place in our reality but was instead a very original, mental implantation hiding from the witness the real events of that night?

Quotation sources

Piotr Cielebiaś' and Michał Kuśnierz's Archives / infra.org.pl

Arek Miazga's Archive / arekmiazga.blogspot.com

Damian Trela's Archive / czastajemnic.blogspot.com

Piechota K., Rzepecki B., *UFO nad Polską*, Białystok 1996.

SOME FINAL WORDS

I T'S very hard to summarise a ufological book especially if the most important things have already been said.

The search for real UFOs and the intelligence (or whatever) that control it is not confined to governments alleged secret knowledge and conspiracies. In fact it is encrypted in thousands of experiences people undergo annually and the ways in which the UFO encounter changes their lives.

We deal with a phenomenon that is magical and absurd, technical and paranormal but the most important thing is that it is beyond the mere human's ability to understand it. Keeping in mind all the different aspects of the UFO phenomenon, one must wonder whether the form it presents to witnesses is real or it is just one disguises the phenomenon is able to adopt in a seemingly chaotic, indecipherable operation.

I do not want to repeat Dr. Vallée's opinions but the cases I have presented in this book, combined with other analyses and comparisons, show that the reality of the UFO phenomenon extends beyond *flying saucers* and the extraterrestrial hypothesis. Its importance and problematic aspects are not confined to the search for extraterrestrial intelligence and national security threats the objects allegedly pose. In other words, although the possibility of alien visitation cannot be excluded, the collection of other experiences deemed ufological in nature may stem from many different sources.

If you are looking to disagree with my point of view may I respectfully suggest that you just do a simple analysis of the UFO phenomenon. You will see that it is hard to find two cases with identical objects or humanoids. They always differ. You also would not find any rational answer why alleged UFO occupants always take humanoid forms and walk the Earth freely. The same applies to their lack of direct contact and the many absurd actions carried out by them.

But there is one outstanding fact: the UFO phenomenon does exist and it is at work. What that work might be is still a mystery. Thus our short trip through Polish UFO history comes to an end. I hope that some of the cases I have featured have at least triggered your curiosity prompting you to ponder what is the real origin and nature of the phenomenon. But remember that UFO truth is just a cheap slogan and there can be numerous truths.

This is only a small section from the Polish annals of strange events that took place over nearly eight decades. What I have provided in this book is in essence an introduction to the amazing events haunting a small country in the heart of Europe – land of high strangeness (in more ways than one).

Piotr Cielebiaś

Lightning Source UK Ltd.
Milton Keynes UK
UKOW06f1722031016

284381UK00029B/825/P